The Complete Book of Beans

The Complete Book of Beans

Jacqueline Hériteau

HAWTHORN BOOKS, INC.
Publishers / NEW YORK
A Howard & Wyndham Company

THE COMPLETE BOOK OF BEANS

Library of Congress Catalog Card Number: 77–92314
ISBN: 0–8015–1474–6
1 2 3 4 5 6 7 8 9 10

This book is for young cooks, like Ruth Macguire's four beautiful daughters: Karen, the nutritionist; Carlie, the carpenter; Corinne, the designer; Chrissie, the madcap; and for my son Kris, the politician—kids whose goal is a brave new world based on real values—and it is for older cooks who, like Ruth, believe that sound nutrition and food that tastes good are part of the love that produces happy, healthy, energetic families.

Contents

Acknowledgments

The subject of beans is amazingly vast, and without the help of experts, the author would have been more perplexed than she was. Among those I wish to thank for their generous donation of time and materials are Doris Hebert and the staff of the California Dry Bean Advisory Board; Pacific Kitchens; the creative and testing agent for the Idaho Bean Commission; Dr. Louis B. Rockland, Research Chemist with the U.S. Department of Agriculture; the Kerr Glass Manufacturing Corporation and the Ball Corporation. I am also very grateful to Helen McCully of *House Beautiful*, who helped track down elusive sources; and for recipes I wish to thank Sally Larkin Erath, author of *Cooking for Two*; Patricia Gill, who wrote the novel about St. Croix entitled *Buddhoe*; the gardening and cooking Hériteau clan in Canada and France. I would also like to thank Sandy Choron of Hawthorn Books for her faith in the project, and Maxine Krasnow for the long hours she put in deciphering the manuscript and getting it into presentable form. To Peter Kalberkamp goes my real gratitude for the handsome drawing appearing at the beginning of each chapter.

1

The Mighty Bean

How could we have failed to suspect the wonder of beans all these years? These days, when protein sources like meat are out of sight in cost and fish is getting there, the only way out seems to be smaller portions on the plate of both these luxuries, and how do you replace them? With bare lettuce leaves and peanut butter? My kids have been brought up in the tradition of food fanciers. So have their closest friends. For instance, Evan Morris at two would pick out and eat the cheese in Roquefort dressing. At twenty-four, Evan knows French wines better than several experts I can name. My own children at a very early age were corrupted from hot dogs to lobsters while visiting the Morrises one summer in Maine. I think Holly was about nine months old at the time.

No, when you love good food, naked lettuce leaves and peanut butter aren't the answer to high protein costs. Nor are heaps of vegetables. We love vegetables, particularly those grown in our garden. But even a plate of the tastiest tomatoes won't leave you feeling full for long—except when the vegetables are the legumes called shell beans and soybeans, all members of the pea family. And thereby hangs this book.

The bean and beanlike legumes included here are several common beans (*Phaseolus vulgaris*); lima beans (*Phaseolus luna-*

tus); blackeye beans, or cowpeas (*Vigna unguiculata*); and garbanzos, or chick-peas (*Cicer arietinum*). These are hereinafter referred to as shell beans: beans grown to be shelled and eaten either fresh, frozen, canned, or dry and cooked.

The other beans included are snap beans, both green and yellow, which also belong to the common bean species, *Phaseolus vulgaris*; and soybeans, *Glycine soya*, which are in a class by themselves. (More about these categories later on.)

Eat a heap of any of these, except the snap beans perhaps, and you do feel full, rather rapidly, and for some time to come. All for good reasons: The shell beans are solid with protein, carbohydrates, and fiber, which give you that comfortably full feeling. Most other vegetables are mainly fluid and leave you feeling the way you do shortly after a good Chinese dinner. Shell beans are solid nutritionally, too, particularly when it comes to protein and iron. Our major sources of protein in the past have been meats, poultry, fish, eggs, and milk products. But beans, in addition to protein, provide fiber, which creates the gentle roughage important to good digestion.

Though they're solid in nutrition, shell beans aren't all that solid in calories. The United States Department of Agriculture rates one cooked serving of 3½ to 4 ounces (100 grams) at 111 to 118 calories, depending on the bean variety. The same amount of steak gives you a handsome 465 calories. Beans (except soybeans) are notably low in fat, have no cholesterol, and are even believed by some to be helpful in reducing cholesterol content.

The USDA reports the following: "Beans are worth their weight in protein, and exceed peanut butter in protein content." For decades peanut (a legume) butter has been a mother's answer to quick nutritional luncheons and snacks. Let's explore ways in which dry shell beans can be the answer to nutritional dinners now that food costs are going up so fast. Big food for small money—that's one of the wonders of beans.

Protein is one of the essential ingredients in the human diet. The total protein available in the world today in relation to global needs presents us with what the experts call the protein problem. Agencies in the U.S. State Department's Food for Peace program have been spearheading a drive to make all nations aware of the need for improving protein quantity and quality. In 1972 the Protein Advisory Board of the United Nations sponsored a symposium in Rome on world protein needs. It was attended by nutritionists who focused on food legume research projects. Beans are legumes. The Subcommittee on Food Legumes, a task force assembled to conduct a protein resource study for the National Science Foundation, reported that about 20 percent of the protein currently available is derived from legumes. Furthermore, they predicted that this source will become even more important in the future.

BEANS AND NUTRITION

Since so many people are banking on beans and bean products, knowing what they mean to you in terms of nutrition has some real value.

Edible legumes contain the highest protein content of all commercial seed crops, but the physical and chemical characteristics vary from legume to legume. The crude protein content of the bean group of legumes runs from 20 to 25 percent, but the protein (actually made up of twenty-two amino acids) is deficient in the amino acid methionine—a fallibility that can be corrected by including in the meal small amounts of fish, poultry, meat, eggs, and milk products. (Meats contain an excess of this amino acid.)

Recently, researchers have come to the conclusion that rice, corn, and wheat, either cooked with shell beans or served with them at the same meal, also enhance and improve the quality of the bean protein. So, you'll find that lots of the bean recipes given here include meat, cheese, corn, rice, or wheat. Recipes that don't include any of these can be made more nutritious if you include in the meal a serving of corn bread or muffins, rice, butter, cheese, milk, or eggs. A dash of grated Parmesan goes well with any shell bean dish containing tomato and with lots that don't. Wheat is easy to include if you make whole-wheat or bran muffins or serve wheat bread.

Shell beans and near beans (such as blackeyes and yellow eyes) are also among the richest natural sources for several of the important B complex vitamins. Cooked blackeye beans are comparable in folic acid content to cooked liver and raw wheat germ. Cooked large lima beans compare favorably with beef liver in respect to thiamin. Average 6-ounce portions of cooked large lima, blackeye, and pink beans represent better sources for pyridoxine (and taste a lot better) than the usual supplement, 1 tablespoon of Brewers yeast or raw wheat germ. A similar serving of cooked dry beans can supply as much as 40 percent of the minimum daily requirement for thiamin and pyridoxine and a significant supplement of niacin as well.

Thiamin and riboflavin are members of the B vitamin complex, and these are found, in varying quantities, in shell beans. Thiamin turns food into energy, keeps nerves healthy, and makes you cheerful. It also has some effect on appetite and digestion. Riboflavin works with thiamin to keep the digestive and nervous systems in good shape and is also good for your eyes and skin.

Niacin is present in larger quantities in the raw beans, but there is some left even after cooking; it helps body cells produce energy and is important to the digestive system, the nerves, and the skin.

Shell beans are a rich source of iron, used to build red blood cells, which carry oxygen from the lungs all around the body. A cup of cooked or canned shell beans provides almost half the iron a man needs daily and about one quarter of the iron a woman needs.

Calcium and phosphorous build bones and teeth and regulate body processes. Baked beans prepared with molasses have a high calcium value.

Potassium, which regulates fluid balances in the body, is plentiful in shell beans, and this is of special interest to people on diuretic medication and for whom low-sodium, high-potassium diets are prescribed. Dietitians are encouraged to specify shell beans as a source of protein for people for whom cholesterol and sodium cause problems.

We do not yet have complete information on the amount and nutritional quality and availability of the important minerals in beans, but we do know that the raw pink beans (those used in much Americanized Mexican cooking) are higher than others in phosphorous, magnesium, calcium, and iron content. Beans also contain traces of vitamins A (butter is high in A and has a whole lot more calories) and C. Fresh snap beans are lower in protein than dry beans, but higher in vitamins A and C. Green beans have more vitamin A, but wax beans have more vitamin B_2. The fresh snap bean has less protein than fresh shell beans. Some say soybeans have everything we've thought of and some things we haven't.

A lot of research is currently underway to find out more about shell beans, since what we know now is incomplete. However, a glimpse into the data available is provided in Tables 1, 2, 3, and 4 from the California Dry Bean Advisory Board's booklet, *Nutritional Values of Dry Bean Varieties Grown in California*, published for members of the American Dietetic Association.

ECONOMY

Dry shell beans are everywhere. Always available in super-markets, today the health food stores and nutrition shops also carry a wondrous assortment. For the most part, the beans cook quickly, although bean cooking times are variable, and there's no way to tell from looking at them whether they'll take the amount of time that I, other cooks, and bean packagers predict. If they're old, they'll take longer. I am still haunted by a letter from a reader who tried a recipe for small white beans in *The Best of Electric Crockery Cooking* and told me that 36 hours later her beans still weren't cooked! I never answered her letter because I didn't know what to say. Some dark red kidney beans I tried once took longer.

The price of well-known brands of beans can be higher than the price of lesser known brands. In the supermarket where I shop brand name dry shell beans cost between fifty and sixty cents a pound (although inflation may have taken its toll by the time you read this). In the same store a pound of dry shell beans sold by a Latin-American producer is in the neighborhood of fifteen cents less per pound. As far as I can judge, the beans are of the same quality. The difference may be that since Latin Americans have always included more beans in their cooking than North Americans, they may sell a lot more beans and therefore may sell them for less.

If you grow and dry your own shell beans, the price of beans is literally beans, especially if you don't take into account the work involved. Yields are hard to pinpoint. Some figures that the U.S. Department of Agriculture (USDA) supplied a few years ago show that ¼ pound of bush shell bean seed will plant a 50-foot row and yield 7 quarts of shell beans. One-half pound of pole shell beans sows a 50-foot row and yields about 10 quarts of shell beans. (See chapter 2.)

In other words, if you serve cooked dry shell beans plain as a vegetable (and some are absolutely delicious that way), the cost is about five to ten cents a portion plus the cost of butter, salt, and the energy used to cook them. You can cook them in a pressure cooker or a slow cooker and bring the energy costs down considerably. Since other vegetables cost close to a dollar for enough to serve four, beans offer a savings of about twenty cents a portion.

Since most of the recipes in this book include with the beans other ingredients such as meat, fish, cheese, butter, rice, corn, wheat, or molasses that enhance the protein and nutritional value of the dish, as well as ingredients to enhance taste, the cost of a bean dinner does go up. If you want to squeeze the budget, you can reduce the proportion of meat (at least one dollar per serving) and increase the proportion of beans (five to ten cents a serving) in the recipes here.

GROWING YOUR OWN

Though both shell and snap beans come in bush varieties, they're essentially climbers, a vertical crop. The shell beans are grown most often as pole-climbers. You can get a lot of pole beans from just enough ground for a tomato bush—say three feet around. They'll climb well from a bushel basket of good rich loam, or an ornate cement urn for that matter. The plants are leafy and green, and in at least one climbing variety, scarlet runner, the flowers (rather like sweet peas) are ornamental as well as food bearing.

Beans also are good for the soil. Most leafy plants remove nitrogen from the ground, but beans, which store nitrogen from the air in their roots, actually contribute nitrogen to the soil. Thus, farmers often follow a bean crop with a leafy crop that needs a lot of nitrogen—lettuce, for instance. This doesn't mean that beans don't need good soil or fertilizing, but it does mean that they can be an asset in planning crop rotation for a healthy garden.

A GLOSSARY OF BEANS

One of the things about shell beans that is confusing and keeps cooks from investigating their potential is that there are so many kinds. I am told there are eighty varieties. The USDA deals primarily with twelve. The Idaho Bean Commission deals with Great Northerns, pintos, small whites, reds, red kidneys, and more. The California Dry Bean Advisory Board describes eight as the number primarily grown commercially there. Recipes usually call for only a few of these beans and often call them by conflicting names. For instance, navy beans are about the same thing as pea beans.

BROAD BEAN: You'll see this broad white or light green bean in lots of early recipes. Horticulturally known as *Vicia fava*, and fava bean, it is the world's third most important bean and is used primarily in Europe. We are offered some types for home gardens in catalogs here, and they are popular in home gardens in Canada and cooler areas.

The bigger forms of broad bean originated in the Mediterranean region, while the smaller types are said to have come from west of the Himalayas. The broad bean won't grow well in hot weather.

COMMON BEAN: *Phaseolus vulgaris* includes the shell beans and snap beans in the Americas. The common bean originated in Central America and South America and was unknown to the rest of the world before the arrival of Columbus.

The twelve most common shell beans for drying are: small white round navy (also called pea) beans; big whites, Great Northerns, and white marrows (also called large whites); small kidney-shaped white (also called navy and pea) beans; pintos (which are patterned in various hues other than the pinto pony's brown on beige); red kidneys (which are light red or dark red, even though there are kidney-shaped beans that are white); pinks (which are the color of light red kidney beans—a sort of a pale, rusty brown-red); small reds (a bit darker than pinks, they are the kind used in Mexico); cranberries (which are similar to small reds); yellow-eye (like blackeye beans, they are also called peas); flat small whites; and black turtles (also simply called blacks, but they are not to be confused with the black beans used in Chinese cooking—those are actually preserved soybeans). Also, a number of shell beans have been developed that are considered almost as good for eating as snap beans when young.

Snap beans are variously called: French beans, string beans, stringless beans, green beans, and wax beans. Wax beans are yellow and green beans are green, but the rest of those names are used in various regions to refer to both or either kind.

Limas, blackeyes, and garbanzos aren't correctly classified as common beans, though they are commonly called shell beans.

SCARLET RUNNER: *Phaseolus coccineus* is the horticultural name since this bean is closely related to the common bean. Seed is offered in some catalogs for home gardens because the plants are so ornamental. The scarlet runner is one of the few plants that climbs from right to left—most climb from left to right. For the gardener with little space, it is of interest because of its fifteen-foot plants with big, showy flowers that produce large coarse pods with red beans. A white-flowered, white-seeded form called White Dutch runner was once grown in some areas of the United States, and the seeds were sold commercially as Oregon lima, or butternut bean. Both kinds are grown in Britain and continental Europe.

LIMA BEAN: Also from Central America, the lima bean is closely related to the common bean. It's another species—*Phaseolus lunatus*—and is grown primarily in the Americas. The small lima (also called baby lima) is grown in the North, since it's the kind that can mature during our shorter growing season. The large lima (also called standard lima, or just "lima") is grown in areas where the season is warm and very long such as California and South America. Though we think of limas as pale green, there are near-whites; and a few types have red or purple patterns. Sometimes you can tell it's a true lima only because it has tiny ridges that radiate from the "eye," the characteristics of a lima.

BLACKEYE: Blackeyes, *Vigna unguiculata sinensis*, are grayish or off-white shell beans, usually with a black "eye." They are called blackeye peas or blackeye beans, but those called blackeye peas in the brand I buy are smaller than blackeye beans. They are also called cowpeas and are referred to in a few areas just as peas, field peas, or southern peas. In spite of the fact that blackeyes are sometimes called peas and aren't really beans at all, the blackeye is more like a bean than a pea. Native to India, it has a very long-podded form with two- to three-foot long pods.

GARBANZOS, or CHICK-PEAS: These knobby fat peas (or beans) are grown as shell beans. The correct horticultural name is

Cicer arietinum. The garbanzo is an annual, grown in California, Mexico, and other Latin areas, though it originally comes from Asia and the Mediterranean. The bushes grow about 24 inches tall and are bushy and rather hairy. Garbanzos are usually dried or canned and take 100 days to mature.

MUNG BEAN: Much used for sprouting, as soybeans, this is *Phaseolus aureus*, another relative of the common bean. It is offered in catalogs for the home gardener. It's native to India, and pods and seeds are smaller than the soybean—only one-eighth inch around. Mung beans are grown extensively in the Orient. I've brought it up because you'll run across the name. We use them primarily for growing bean sprouts, which is described on pages 48–49.

SOYBEAN: Horticulturally *Glycine soya*, this is one of the few beans about which there are relatively few confusions. It is truly a miracle plant, as well as the world's most important legume. It has fed China for thousands of years. Whereas other beans are higher in carbohydrates (starches) than in protein, the soybean is the reverse and is only 35 percent carbohydrate. It has a very high fat content—18 percent—compared to the 1½ percent fat common to other legumes. Soy oil is an important product in the American economy, but there are more than a hundred other products ranging from adhesives to plastics and waterproofing preparations made from soybeans. In the food line, soybeans are used sprouted or made into flour, grits, or flakes. The flour is added to prepared mixes; macaroni, spaghetti, noodles, and other pasta products; soups; cereals; crackers; bakery goods; sausages; meat stretchers; and on and on.

Soy milk, great for infants and those allergic to cow's milk, is made from ground soybeans, as are many products familiar to us from Oriental food shops: bean sprouts, soy sauce, fish sauce, oyster sauce (made from oysters, brine, and soy sauce), red bean paste, and bean curds.

Truly one of the most amazing beans, soybeans grown in the home garden make very good fresh shell beans to be gathered late in the fall. The fresh soybeans can be canned or frozen, as other shell beans, or left on the vines to harvest when dry.

I assume you are now as confused as I was once. Don't try to remember all these names. If you need to, you can look them up in the Index. To simplify and generalize:

• *Soybeans and mung beans* make up the sprouting varieties.
• *Green and wax snap beans* are the kinds most grown for eating in the pod stage.
• *Shell beans* (discussed more fully in the following section) include whites, pintos, pinks, reds, kidneys, blackeyes, blacks, limas, and garbanzos.

These simplifications apply to general cooking procedures. There are lots of cooks who won't forgive the failure to deal with *flageolets*. You can order seed for these French dried beans from gourmet seed specialists, such as J. A. Demonchaux Co., Inc., 827 North Kansas, Topeka, Kansas 66608.

SHELL BEANS

It is my opinion that shell beans are probably the most misunderstood—and therefore largely ignored—of all bean varieties. If confusion about them has contributed to their undeserved fate, the purpose of the following material is to emphasize that shell beans really do belong in the forefront of your culinary imagination.

Before the shrinking food dollar and my interest in vegetables encouraged me to investigate dry shell beans, all I knew about beans was Boston baked; chili con carni; and white beans in *gigot et flageolets*, a dish French food buffs consider special. To anyone whose only knowledge of shell beans is similar, an exploration of flavors will come as a real surprise. I obtained my own education in shell beans by buying one of every package of dry shell beans in the supermarket and cooking a cupful of each. Then I tasted them just-cooked with butter, salt, and pepper, and cold with French dressing. I reheated after refrigeration. I froze and cooked them, canned and cooked them, and mashed and warmed them with butter, salt, and pepper. And I combined them with various leftovers.

Whether they're the small flattish white, round navy (or pea) beans, or the marrow, big whites, or Great Northerns, all white beans have essentially the same flavor. The big ones are buttery, mealy when cooked, and rather bland, like those often used in Boston Baked Beans. You might use them in a meal the way you use mashed potatoes or pastas.

Limas, which are usually pale green kidney-shaped beans, big or small, taste rather like a cross between white beans and fresh green beans. The texture is buttery, and they're great plain with butter, salt, and pepper. They're best known in succotash, a mixture of baby limas and corn. Soybeans taste a little like limas.

Pinto beans, which are usually patterned in brown on beige, are really delicious plain (as good as butternut squash) or served with butter, a little coarse salt, and a grating of fresh black pepper. The flavor is slightly nutty and the texture mealy. Cooked pintos look like cooked pink beans.

Pink beans are similar to pintos and again may be served plain or with butter, salt, and pepper. These are the beans used most often in American Mexican dishes. In authentic Mexican cooking, however, a small red bean, tough and strongly flavored, is used.

Red beans—whether red, cranberry, small red, light red, light red kidney, or dark red kidney—are usually stronger in flavor (rather nutty) than pintos, pinks, or whites. I also find that the skins are tougher. Light red kidney beans are those used by many southern homemakers to make chili; as they cook more quickly than the dark red kidneys used in commercial chili.

Yellow eyes, which are a common bean, *Phaseolus vulgaris*, and blackeye beans, *Vigna unguiculata sinensis*, are not especially interesting when served plain. But there are lots of combination dishes in which these are particularly good.

Garbanzos, or chick-peas, *Cicer arietinum*, have a nutty flavor all their own, and are not usually served plain, except in Italian antipasto plates.

Black beans have a very strong flavor, rather like the equally colorful reds. I don't recommend these plain, but there are dishes for which they are absolutely essential. They are a good replacement, as you will see in the section on black bean recipes, for a red bean used in Spain, and are the key ingredient in Black Bean Soup (pages 160–161), which is delicious.

One advantage to sampling each different variety plain is that this will give you a notion of things you can do with each kind and an understanding of how they cook up. It also suggests which beans can be used as replacement for others in various bean recipes. In the chapters that follow I have proposed alternative beans within the recipes. But if you know what they taste like naturally, you'll have ideas of your own for the use of leftovers and may be inspired to create and adapt your own recipes.

Tip: When you're serving cooked dry shell beans plain as a vegetable, it pays to cook them especially for the occasion. Although cooked shell beans keep in the refrigerator and freeze and stay canned well, they really are best plain just after being cooked.

Shell beans are used fresh as well as dry. Some varieties can be picked young and eaten as snap beans. As soon as they're developed enough to have good-size beans in the pods, they can be shelled and cooked fresh (fresh limas and blackeyes are two that are nicer fresh than dry). In areas where the climate allows the garden to produce beans over a very long season, the shell beans are often preferred fresh.

SHELL BEAN QUANTITIES

Even when you are giving dry shell beans indoor storage space, they're practical. One cup of dry beans, cooked, serves two to four; 1 quart serves two to four meals for four; 10 quarts serves twenty to forty meals for four. (One 50-foot row yields enough beans to serve one four-person family one bean meal a week for 20 to 40 weeks.) And they need relatively little storage space. Compare how much space spinach, or carrots, for forty meals would require!

Dry shell beans offer other practicalities, too. They take a while to cook right, but you can cook 1 quart of dry shell beans—enough for four meals for two to four—almost as easily as you can cook 1 cupful. Once cooked, they keep well for a week or 10 days in the refrigerator, or frozen in their own cooking liquid (divided into 1-cup lots), 12 months.

Shell beans are also good "meal stretchers": Take a tag end of boeuf bourguignon that has lots of good gravy but little meat left, add an 8-ounce can of tomato sauce and 2 cups of cooked pink or pinto beans, and you have a delicious main dish for four. Add the pinks or pintos to the meat sauce remnants, along with a teaspoon of chili powder, and you have a very good mock chili con carne. You can add any of the whites or limas to creamed chicken leftovers and to soups, too. The variations on this scheme are many, and all are good.

2

Beans in the Garden

If you've never grown beans, the two bits of information you need before you can choose a suitable variety are (1) that snap, shell, and lima beans grow on low bushes as well as on climbing vines; and (2) that both kinds of beans, bush beans and pole beans (the climbers), come in early, midseason, and late varieties. Early beans mature in about 50 days; midseasons take 60 to 75. The late beans, which take about 95 to 120 days, are big limas and shell-type pole beans. As a rule the bigger the end product, the longer the time it takes to mature.

Bush plants produce fewer beans per plant but mature more quickly. When I have a lot of gardening space, I grow bush snap beans, which I happen to think are generally finer in flavor; and they're easier to grow and pick, since they don't require poles. When limited to small gardening spaces, such as terraces, I grow climbing, or pole-type, snap beans. When I have *very* little space for beans, I grow only green snap beans, my favorites.

Pole beans are my choice when I am growing shell beans for drying, because then I want a big harvest, and these, I think, produce more.

When it comes to choosing varieties, I've made a few suggestions further on, but not many. Each year the catalogs offer new variations on good old bean names, and keeping up with them is impossible. Furthermore, some beans do better in some regions than do others, and the only people who really know which are resistant to local problems and thrive on local virtues are the local gardeners, the local garden supply centers, and the Cooperative Agricultural Extension Service usually located at your state university.

PREPARING THE SOIL

Beans, especially pole beans, respond best to rich garden soil that is loamy in structure and well worked. They don't like an excessively acid soil.

The symbol *pH* refers to the acidity or alkalinity of the soil. Neutral is 7.0 on a pH scale. Below that number is acid, above is alkaline. Vegetables respond best to soil whose pH is between 6.0 and 6.8. Soils whose original wildings were blueberries or evergreens are probably acid. If the growth was richly green, compact, and growing sturdily, chances are the soil is either just right for beans or maybe a shade too sweet (alkaline).

To find out what the pH really is in the spot you've chosen for your garden, buy a reasonably priced soil-testing kit and follow its directions. Or you may send a sample of the soil to the Agricultural Extension Service. The testing kit or the Extension Service will tell you how much lime to add if the soil needs sweetening and how much ammonium sulfate (or variation thereof) to add if the soil is too alkaline.

I can't say exactly which fertilizing combination you should use on your soil, since soils differ. If the pH is right, any balanced commercial fertilizer should be appropriate.

The rate of usage is usually 50 pounds for a garden 2,500 square feet—that's a big garden, say 50 feet square, or 100 feet by 25 feet. For a garden half or a quarter that size, proportion the dose. Don't add more fertilizer, or anything else, than you need. A stew with twice as much salt as the recipe calls for doesn't taste better.

The terms *good garden loam* or *friable soil* refers to soils that are loose and fluffy, easy for tiny plant roots to grow through. Soil has three main elements: sand, clay, and humus. Good garden loam's soil structure is perfect for vegetables and is composed of these three elements in equal proportions. If humus is missing, the soil fails to retain the moisture plants need in order to grow. When sand is missing, soils bake hard and won't let water or air in or through. When clay is missing, nutrients are scarce.

To test your soil structure, take up a handful on a day when the soil is damp—not soggy—and press it between your hands as though making a snowball. If the soil balls easily and crumbles readily under slight pressure from your thumb, it is probably right. If the ball falls apart and won't stick, the soil may contain too much sand. If the ball won't break, there is probably too much clay. To correct soil structure, add whichever of these elements is missing, in whatever quantity is needed.

To judge these quantities, clear a one-foot square of space and add layers one at a time (an inch at a time) of the elements you believe are missing. Dig each layer into the soil 18 inches deep, then test again. Keep a record of what it takes to get your test patch right, multiply it by the area to be planted, and order what you need from the garden supply center.

SOILS FOR POTTED BEANS

Pole beans grow very well in containers filled with rich soil. If you have it, use good garden loam and fertilizer as you would in the open garden. Or, mix your own potting soil by the bushel. Use one part peat moss, two parts garden soil or ordinary bagged potting soil, and two parts sand or vermiculite or perlite. Vermiculite and perlite are lighter than sand and are recommended when the weight of large containers must be considered. For each bushel of this mixture, mix in 9 level tablespoons of superphosphate, 1 level tablespoon of cottonseed meal, 4 level tablespoons sulfate of potash, and 2 level tablespoons of ground limestone.

COMPOST

The term *organic gardening* describes the way we *used* to garden when a horse-and-buggy society made manure available. Organic garden buffs use natural (defined "as found in nature") vegetable and mineral additives and their derivatives for fertilizers. Instead of using pesticides, they try to attract or even breed the plant's natural allies, birds, and may import beneficial insects. As for diseases, organic gardeners claim a record of considerable immunity to disease as a result of growing plants in soil with correct pH balances, natural fertilizers, and good structure.

A major ally of the organic gardener is compost used as fertilizer, soil improver, and humus. Compost is organic material that has decomposed in soil.

The basic method for composting is to layer together organic materials (grass clippings, leaves, seaweed) with soil. If you add lime and fertilizers to the compost pile as you construct it, the compost will be fertile. A key in the composting process is the humidity in the soil. To speed the process, the pile is turned weekly, monthly, or seasonally, depending on ambition and energy.

A simple method of making a compost pile is this: Strip the sod from a 3-, 4-, or 5-foot square somewhere out of sight, dig a pile of soil from the area, and set it to one side. During the coming season, as vegetative wastes and garbage become available, make layers. Start with a 6-inch layer of refuse, cover it either with a 3-inch layer of manure (fresh or old, or a 1-inch layer of dried) or with a 3-inch layer of soil (any kind) into which you mix 1 pound of complete garden fertilizer. Build the layers so that they are concave and will catch and hold rainwater. Continue to add layers until the end of the season or until the pile is 5 feet high. If you turn the pile every few weeks, it will compost (decompose the organic materials) more quickly. You can also add commercial products that hasten the process.

There are, of course, simpler methods of composting. For instance, you can compost in garbage cans and large heavy-duty plastic bags. Buy a starter product that hurries decomposition, and follow directions carefully. You will also find in catalogs small composting units such as heavy-duty mesh bins with support posts that will hold about 50 to 60 bushels of leaves.

DIGGING A NEW GARDEN

If you are gardening where no garden has been before, tilling (stirring or turning the soil) will be necessary. First measure the garden and mark it out carefully and neatly with strings and pegs. Then strip the sod and all growth from the soil before you turn it in order to prevent weeds that propagate by means of underground runners from getting plowed under (these can breed descendants for years to come). If the area is larger than 10 feet by 10 feet, rent a rototiller or have it rototilled, but in either case, remove the sod first; this must be done by hand. With a flat-edge spade, make squares 1 foot by 1 foot; cut down into the sod around each square; then with the spade or with a spading fork dig under the square and lift it.

Before you till, spread manure or slow-release fertilizer over the soil, and add soil improvers, such as compost.

If a rototiller isn't indicated, turn the soil by hand. This process is called double-digging. To double-dig, remove one spadeful of soil, about 8 by 10 inches deep, and lift it onto the soil surface ahead of you. Then lift a clump 8 by 10 inches deep from below the first one and place it beside the first one. Move back a few steps, dig under, and lift a top clump of soil, turn it upside down into the hole ahead, spank it—that is, hit it hard to break it up— then lift and shake it to remove loose soil, and slide into a wheelbarrow any knotted weeds holding together. (Later, the wheelbarrow contents can go to the compost pile.) Lift a second level clump from the hole just in front of you, turn it upside down into the first hole, repeat the spanking and shaking process, and discard what remains. Continue until the whole garden has been dug and fluffed.

When digging or rototilling is finished, rake the garden smooth with a steel rake, removing surface pebbles and dying weeds. Now you are almost ready to plant.

PLANTING THE ROWS

Beans, whether pole or bush, growing in neat rows are prettier and more satisfying than beans growing in crooked rows. To make rows straight, I make a peg line, a sturdy string tied to two pointed wooden pegs about 6 inches high. I poke a peg into the soil at each end of the row. Then I pull the string taut around one peg so that the string lines up with the square of the garden. I plant under the string.

Beans of the bush type are planted in rows 20 to 30 inches apart. In New England the farmers I've known plant them in rows that are 20 inches apart. When the bushes mature, the leaves meet between rows, shadowing the soil and inhibiting weeds. This old-fashioned method saves space while the canopy of leaves acts as a mulch and helps keep roots cool.

Another way is to plant rows 30 inches apart, with the idea that you can use a small hand- or machine-driven tiller to root up the weeds between the rows, air the soil, and decompact it. Walking between rows tends to compact the soil. When there's space of this sort between rows, you can mulch with shredded leaves or seaweed or rotted hay (usually sold for very little, if available) or buck-wheat hulls (expensive) to keep down the weeds.

Plant bush-type seeds 3 to 5 inches apart, either in drills or in hills. *Drills* is a gardener's word for rows of vegetables. (Neat, single-file rows look like soldiers at drill?) *Hills* is a gardener's word for groups; in this case, groups of six, later thinned to four seedlings. If you are planting in drills, then the rows can be closer together. If you are planting in hills, then there must be greater distance between the rows. Plant seeds 2 to 3 inches apart for drills and hills. As the seedlings grow, thin the plants to stand 3 to 5 inches apart. When you thin them, remove the weakest plants.

The depth for planting bush bean types is about 1½ inches. If you are planting in a drill, drag the top of a pointed hoe down the row beneath the string (that keeps it straight) to make a furrow about 1½ inches deep. Walk back down the row dropping seeds 2 to 3 inches apart; then use the rake or the hoe to shove loose soil back over the furrow so that the seeds are about 1 inch deep. If you are planting in hills, make six planting holes in a circle with the handle or business end of a trowel 5 to 7 inches apart and 1½ inches deep. Plant the seeds and cover with 1 inch of soil. Later, thin the seeds to stand 8 to 10 inches apart.

Plant pole beans in holes 2 to 3 inches deep and cover with 1 inch of soil. Plant them in a circle, six seeds around each pole, 10 to 12 inches apart, eventually thinning to four seedlings. Set the poles about 20 inches apart.

Plant bean seeds—especially limas—eye (inner curve) down. That's where roots begin.

STAKING POLE BEANS

Stakes for pole beans come in many styles; some aren't even poles at all. The single pole and the teepee or tripod pole system are the two most common. If you are using a single pole, it must be sturdy, preferably 2-inch staking lumber. If you are planning a teepee, you can use 2-inch bamboo poles.

Since most pole beans grow 6 to 8 feet tall, poles must be about 6 feet tall, with a good 6 inches buried in the ground so that they are well supported. Set the poles 30 to 36 inches apart.

Some beans are vining plants that naturally grow to a length of only 2½ feet or so. These can be trained to run along a fence of one or two wires supported by short poles about 3 feet from the ground, or on brush stakes. The stakes are planted before the seeds are planted.

WHEN TO PLANT

Beans are planted at the same time as corn: in mid-spring after the ground has warmed—that is, about 3 to 4 weeks after the frost has left the ground and it has become workable. I've always been told to plant corn when the apple blossoms fall, and, except for certain kinds, like the broad bean, which can be planted in March or April, that's a good time to plant beans as well.

VARIETIES TO CONSIDER

Although I can't tell you which bean is best in your area, I can suggest some varieties of general good repute. In addition, you may study catalogs whose descriptions give a notion of qualities to consider when selecting varieties.

For eating fresh, Golden Wax is a bush snap, a heavy bearer that is stringless and of good flavor. Kinghorn Wax is another good yellow bush bean. Tenderpod and Tendercrop are my favorites in bush-style green snap beans for eating fresh, and they endure tougher weather than others. If bean mosaics and mildew are problems (see pages 24–25), choose resistant varieties such as Tendercrop, Wade, and Improved Tendercrop. These are bush types that mature in 55 to 60 days from seed. Brown-seeded or white-seeded Kentucky Wonders are good pole varieties of green snap bean and mature in 60 to 65 days.

Lima beans for eating fresh come in pole and bush varieties. Henderson Bush Lima and Baby Fordhook Bush Lima require 60 to 65 days to mature. Fordhook 42 is a heat-resistant bush lima indicated for the South. Burpee's Improved Bush Lima is a new variety, easier to shell than many. It matures in about 74 days. Pole lima bean varieties such as Prizetaker mature in about 88 days, and the Carolina or Sieva in about 78 days.

For canning and freezing Canyon is a good bush-type green snap bean that matures in about 52 days. It is resistant to mosaics and curly-top virus. Greensleeves, which take 56 days to mature, is another bush green snap bean suggested for canning and freezing. If you want to grow beans up a trellis or along a fence, consider White Half Runner, which takes 60 days to mature. It produces 3- to 4-foot runners that need no other staking. Brittle Wax, 52 days for maturity, and Goldencrop, 54 days, are two more recommended varieties of yellow beans.

Among the pole green and yellow snap varieties, one recommended for canning and freezing is Burpee Golden (60 days to maturity), a tender stringless butter-yellow type. Blue Lake, which is white-seeded and takes 60 days to mature, is popular for canning and freezing. Its small white seeds are also good as shell beans.

Kentucky Wonder, which is great fresh, is also good for freezing. The pods, when small, may be picked for snap beans, or they can be allowed to mature into shell beans. There's a rust-resistant variety of Kentucky Wonder for areas where rust is a problem.

Among beans for shelling and drying, Red Kidney, 95 days to maturity, is a good one for Spanish and Mexican cooking, and grows to about 2 feet tall. Marrowfat is a popular white bean and is considered excellent in baked dishes. Choices of varieties among other kinds and colors of shell beans are numerous. Read the catalogs and consult the local Agricultural Extension Service for varieties most successful in your area.

Among the bush lima beans, some to consider for canning or freezing are Fordhook (75 days to maturity), also called "potato" lima, which grow on plants 24 inches across and about 20 inches tall. Baby Fordhook Bush Lima (65 days to maturity) is a small type billed as a potato lima—very mealy—that grows on bushes only 14 inches tall. Henderson Bush Lima (65 days to maturity) is earlier yet, a buttery baby lima for canning and freezing and excellent for drying.

Among the pole lima beans, which take about 90 days to mature, Prizetaker has exceptionally large beans, is excellent for freezing, and yields a lot of beans per pod—that means less shelling. Burpee's Best, which takes a few days longer to mature, is recommended as giving a higher yield per plant than many others. It's a strong climber that will go to 10 to 12 feet, with mealy potato-type beans.

Kanrich is a soybean ready to eat as a shell bean in about 105 days and is good for freezing. Burgess is one of many catalogs I have that offer both soy and mung bean seed for the home gardener. Burgess is located in Galesburg, Michigan, 49053; see chapter 6 for more information about growing soybeans and mung beans.

INOCULATING BEAN SEEDS

According to experts, you should inoculate beans—that is, treat the seeds with a nitrogen-fixing bacteria—if they are being planted in a new garden or in a garden whose soil is less than really fertile.

Inoculating is a relatively simple procedure. Some state universities sell inoculant at cost; and commercial seed companies sell it as well. Package directions should be followed carefully. Be sure, however, that the inoculant you purchase is this year's supply.

WATERING

If possible, plant beans the days after a rain. After planting, water the row lightly, with a fine spray, disturbing the soil above the seeds as little as possible. A downpour from the hose can remove the soil covering and dislodge the beans. In moist soil, seeds will sprout in just a few days if the weather is warm.

Beans need a thorough watering weekly. A light spray every day encourages shallow roots that might otherwise be caught out in later droughts. Water with a soaker if that's possible. Wet bean leaves seem vulnerable to a number of diseases. Don't brush against wet bean plants—the flowers drop like ninepins, and there goes the crop.

FERTILIZING

Bush beans growing in well-fertilized garden loam shouldn't need additional fertilizer. But pole beans and lima beans stay in the ground longer, have more work to do, and are bigger plants to feed. So, when their blossoms appear, work 1 tablespoon of 4–8–4 or a handful of fertile compost into the ground in each hill or around each plant. Don't get the fertilizer right next to the roots, as some types can harm the roots.

MULCHING AND WEEDING

Planting bush beans close together so that the mature leaves will create a shade for the earth and act as an inhibitor to weeds is one way of mulching beans. Another is to fill the ground surface around the plants with mulch—leaves, grass clippings, buckwheat hulls, seaweed, rotten hay—almost anything organic will do; or use plastic mulches—garden centers sell rolls of dark plastic for this purpose. The organic mulch performs several functions: It keeps weeds down, stops evaporation, keeps roots cool, and as it decomposes, it adds humus to the soil. The plastic mulch keeps weeds out and moisture in.

Lay a mulch after the seeds have sprouted. If you fill the rows with organic mulch earlier, the mulch may drift and cover the sprouts. To keep weeds down while waiting for the sprouts, rake the soil lightly every few days. The few weeds that come up right in around the sprouts can be scraped away carefully with a hoe later, or they may be pulled up by hand if they're too close to be hoed. If weeds get a real start, you can cut them down with a sharp hoe.

If you have planted bush beans close so they can mulch themselves later, weed till the leaves have closed over the space between the rows. Rake tiny weeds; hoe down big ones.

If your garden is new, it pays to control weeds around it. If weeds go to seed, the seeds will fly to your carefully prepared, rich, welcoming garden soil, and next season they'll sprout faster than the beans you planted.

HARVESTING

Keep the plants of the beans to be eaten fresh, picked clear of maturing beans, and they'll produce over a longer period. Once a plant starts putting its energy into growing seeds in the pods, it loses interest in producing more flowers, so bean production drops.

Pick green beans when they are 6 to 8 inches in length. That's when they taste best. Pick yellow beans when still young, right after the pods have turned a good strong yellow. Pick shell beans to be eaten as pods, fresh, when the pods are still flattish and look like green beans. Pick shell beans to be eaten fresh when the pods begin to swell out and the growing beans inside are becoming visible. Snap them off just below the stem end.

Let shell beans for drying dry on the vine. When the leaves have fallen and the pods are browning, the dried beans are ready for harvesting. One method for securing the beans, recommended by a soybean grower, is to cut or pull up the plants, put them in a big plastic bag, and beat the bag. That breaks the brittle pods and loosens the beans, which are tough enough to stand up to a beating. Another method is to pick the pods and spread them out on screens (window screens will do) to dry in the sun. Bring them in when evening moisture begins to be felt. When the pods are crackling dry, shell them, spread the beans on shallow cookie trays, one layer deep, and dry the beans quickly in a low oven—250 degrees Fahrenheit for about 10 minutes. Store them in cardboard boxes, sealed jars, or plastic bags. Check the containers the first few weeks; if you see signs of mildew or any hint of moisture, discard spoiled beans and repeat the drying process. A cool, dry place is the best storage area.

BEAN PROBLEMS

Beans growing in good garden loam, well fertilized, watered, and cared for, don't have too many problems. However, there are a few you might keep an eye out for.

ANTHRACNOSE: The symptoms are round dark sunken spots on the pods, pink in the center. Avoid touching the plants when moist (this spreads disease), and in the future use Western seed.

BACTERIAL BLIGHT: Symptoms are brown areas on the leaves and red-brown spots on the pods. Don't touch the plant when moist, and use Western seed next season.

MOSAICS: Stunted plants and yellow mottling of the leaves are the symptoms. I've run into this one, and the solution is to control the aphids, which spread the disease, by using Malathion according to the manufacturer's directions. Next season plant mosaic resistant varieties.

MEXICAN BEAN BEETLE: The leaves are reduced to skeletons. You can't miss the symptom. I've had this, too. Control the beetles with rotenone dust.

BEAN WEEVIL: These show up in the stored dried beans. Next season use treated seed.

DOWNY MILDEW: This shows up as white mold on the pods of lima beans. I've had this one, too. Treat plants weekly with Maneb or Zineb, and examine the branch crotches carefully to make sure you're treating everything.

The controls I've suggested are recommended by the Connecticut Agricultural Extension Service as safe. Your local Extension Service and garden centers may have other products that are considered safe and have given good results in your area.

Garden rows in which beans have had problems are not good places to plant next year's crop. Crop rotation is one way gardeners keep their gardens healthy. Diseases and pests tend to be specific to one genus and its species and varieties, and their remains in this year's row tend to prey on next year's crop. If you switch crops, it discourages them.

Locating your garden in an airy place is another good health measure. Damp, hot, airless corners are ideal breeding grounds for everything that's bad. Again, avoid wetting bean leaves, if you can. And don't handle diseased plants when they are wet. Rather, deal with them when they are dry.

3

Beans in the Freezer

A freezer full of beans—that's easier to achieve and handier than you can imagine.

Freezing snap beans is worthwhile because of their flavor. If the beans are pencil-slim and fresh from your garden, after freezing they really are as good as fresh beans, though the texture isn't quite as crisp.

When the bean crop is plentiful, the easiest thing in the world is to prepare extras for freezing while cooking the beans to be used for a dinner. This few-at-a-time method is a painless way to freeze and adds only a few more minutes to the time it takes to prepare fresh beans for one meal.

Freezing is considered the handiest way to put up shell beans, whether they're fresh or dry and cooked. When you cook with fresh-picked shell beans, pick enough from the garden to freeze one batch. When you cook dry shell beans, cook enough to make one extra meal and freeze the extras.

I generally freeze shell beans in 1-cup lots, for just 1 cup of cooked beans can be enough to stretch leftover stews or soups and rice.

Leftover bean stew, by the way, freezes beautifully, whereas carrots and potatoes in similar stews thaw out to a mealy consistency.

EQUIPMENT FOR FREEZING

The only equipment you need for freezing is a kettle big enough to blanch the beans in, freezer containers, and of course, a freezer.

Containers are important. If any air gets at foods inside the freezer, the food may become dehydrated and taste terrible.

For limas and shell beans, I use small square plastic containers. They're easy to work with and can be washed in the dishwasher (although I do the lids by hand because the heat of the dishwasher often causes them to warp). In my area, the most readily available are 1- and 3-cup sizes. Three cups is just enough beans and/or stew or soup for my family of four.

If you are going to put snap beans up in quantities, the handiest freezer containers are those made of waxed cardboard, or plastic, in rectangular shapes similar to commercial frozen bean packages. This is a good shape for snap beans frozen whole, because the beans can lie flat and straight in a neat bundle. They come out of the package unbroken, and once they are placed in boiling water, they are easy to separate—easier than if they've been frozen tangled up.

If you don't have proper freezer containers, improvise. Glass jars will do as long as the sides aren't curved and they allow ¼ to ½ inch headroom above the beans. Plastic bags, overwrapped in freezer-duty foil or paper, are fine, too, as are coffee tins with plastic lids if you line them with plastic bags.

FREEZING TIME

How long will bean foods retain optimum flavor and nutritional value in the freezer? The Ball Corporation, manufacturers of canning equipment, suggest that blanched beans will last 12 months, while cooked-through beans will last 1 month; prepared casseroles, soups, and stews last for 6 months. That's at freezer temperatures that stay at 0 degrees Fahrenheit. Naturally, you should use frozen packages in the order in which they were stored.

THAWING TIME

The amount of time necessary for a frozen package to thaw depends on the size of the package. Withdraw frozen soups and stews from the freezer the night before you plan to use them and allow them to thaw in the refrigerator. Before preparing the meal the next day, the package may be left out on the kitchen counter to finish thawing. Unwrapped and set near the stove where something is cooking, beans in 1-cup lots usually will thaw in an hour or so. You can also free a frozen block of beans from its container and add it directly to a simmering stew or soup; it will thaw in 10 to 15 minutes.

To cook a 1-cup quantity of frozen snap beans and limas, set ½ cup of water over high heat, and when it is boiling rapidly, turn the frozen beans into the water. Leave the saucepan uncovered until the water returns to a boil; then with two forks gently break apart the beans. Cover the pan, lower the heat, and simmer until the beans are just tender, usually about 4 to 7 minutes.

FREEZING SNAP AND OTHER EDIBLE-POD BEANS

If possible, pick slender beans of the same size and harvest just before you are ready to freeze. Snip off the stem ends and sort the beans according to thickness. If some of the beans are old and thick, slice them lengthwise down the center—but not down the seam. Beans cut this way are known as French-style beans.

When you are freezing fresh, raw beans, they must be blanched before they are put into the freezer. Blanching—a quick trip in boiling water—stops enzyme action that causes further growth and ripening. The process also softens the beans a little, makes them easier to pack into the freezer containers and quickens their cooking later.

If you are planning to freeze snap beans in small lots—1 or 2 pounds—set the blanching water to boil before you pick the beans. If you are doing a large lot of snap beans—4 or 5 pounds—pick and wash the beans; and when you have the tips and ends snipped off half the batch, set the blanching water to boil. Then proceed as follows:

If you are freezing shell beans fresh, pick, wash, and shell the beans before you start boiling water.

1. Fill a 6-quart kettle that has a lid with 4 quarts of water

and set it to boil over high heat. Four quarts of water will accommodate about 4 cups of beans.

2. While the water is coming to a boil, prepare the vegetables, discarding any spoiled or imperfect beans, and get the containers ready.

3. Fill the sink with water and ice.

4. If you have a wire basket with a handle, place the prepared vegetables, 4 cups at a time, into it. A colander is a fair substitute. Place the basket of vegetables into the rapidly boiling water. Put the lid on the kettle immediately and start counting the blanching time. Blanch whole slim young beans for exactly 3 minutes. Blanch very thin or French-cut beans for 1 minute. Blanch whole large beans cut into 1- or 2-inch pieces 2 minutes. (For time of fresh limas and other shell beans, succotash, and cooked dry shell beans, see the following sections.)

5. As soon as the blanching time is up, lift the basket or colander from the water and plunge it into the iced water. Count out exactly the same number of minutes as you did for blanching. Remove the beans, drain them, and spread them on paper towels to dry out a little.

6. Fill the cardboard and plastic freezer containers as full as possible and put on the lids. The fewer air spaces inside the box the better the beans will be. If the containers are glass, allow ¼ to ½ inch of headroom.

7. Label the beans with name and date.

8. If you have a fast-freezing compartment, place the beans there. If not, place the beans in the coldest spot the freezer affords. Leave some space between packages so that as much icy air as possible surrounds each package while it is freezing.

FREEZING FRESH LIMAS AND OTHER SHELL BEANS

Pick the beans, wash and then shell them. Shelling can take time, especially with limas. If lima pods are tough, plunge them into boiling water for 1 minute, then cool them in the sink in cold water, then pull the string tips down hard to open the pods. Or, use a sharp knife or scissors to snip them open down one side. Sort the shelled beans according to size. Follow the freezing instructions for snap and edible-pod beans (pages 28–29) using the following blanching times:

Blanch larger limas and shell beans for 4 minutes. Blanch medium beans for 3 minutes, and blanch baby limas for 2 minutes.

FREEZING SUCCOTASH

Succotash is a mixture of corn and baby limas, and it's delicious when the beans and corn are fresh from your garden. For every 20 ears of corn you will need 10 cups of shelled lima beans. You can use other types of shell beans to make succotash, but not the red beans nor the blacks. You need a mealy bean, like a buttery large or small white.

Review the instructions given for freezing snap and edible-pod beans (pages 28–29), but adapt the blanching procedure as follows:

1. Husk, remove the silk, and wash the corn. Cover with boiling water and boil for 5 minutes. Remove the corn, reserving the water. Cool the cobs quickly in ice water. Hold the cobs upright, and with a sharp knife, cut the whole kernels cleanly from the cobs. Measure the corn in cup-size batches. For each cup of limas or fresh shell beans, measure out ⅔ cup of corn kernels and turn the corn into a big bowl.

2. Bring the water the corn boiled in back to a boil and plunge the measured limas or shell beans into it. Add more boiling water if needed to bring the water level back up to cover the beans. After the water starts to boil again, count out 3 minutes. Remove the beans and chill them for 3 minutes in the ice water. Drain the beans well, and mix with the corn. Pack in 2-cup containers for the freezer. Seal, label, and then freeze the containers.

FREEZING DRY SHELL BEANS

Wash and pick over the beans, cover them in about three times their volume of water, bring to a boil, boil for 2 minutes, remove from the heat, cover, and let stand 2 hours. (If the beans are quick-cooking kinds that don't need soaking, skip this maneuver.) Return the beans to the heat, bring back to a boil, and then lower the heat and simmer until just slightly underdone (freezing will eventually soften them further). Check the water level often, periodically adding enough liquid to keep the beans covered. As I have said elsewhere, and often, there is no precise cooking timetable possible for dry beans. How long they take to cook depends on altitude, hardness of water, and the length of time the beans have been on the grocer's shelves—or your own. And it also has to do with the actual weather the year they grew. However, in my experience, the limas take 45 minutes to an hour, the blackeyes about an hour, and the others 1 to 2 hours. If you soak the beans overnight, or bring them to a boil in water to cover, boil about 2 minutes, then let stand for an hour (called the quick-soak method). They'll cook more quickly than if you start the beans cooking without soaking.

Set the saucepan containing the beans into a sink filled with cold water and ice, and stir the beans to hurry the cooling. When the beans are cold, pack them into containers; then seal, label, and put them in the freezer following the basic rules for freezing snap and edible-pod beans (pages 28–29).

4

Beans in the Canner

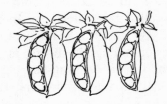

Canned beans taste pretty good, though canning generally requires more work than freezing. Before you consider canning beans, remember that you will need the proper equipment: a pressure canner and real canning jars with proper canning lids.

Canning may be accomplished in a regular pressure cooker but only under certain conditions: To be safe for use as a canner, the ordinary pressure cooker must have a recently checked reliable gauge that registers 10- to 15-pound pressures accurately. You should also be aware that ordinary pressure cookers are only large enough to hold pint jars. Before you start canning, clean the safety valve and the petcock on your pressure canner or cooker. Draw a clean string through the petcock to make sure it is clear. When canning beans in an ordinary pressure cooker, add 20 minutes to the processing times given in the instructions here.

Note: When canning snap beans and fresh beans of any kind, pick the beans only when you are ready to start canning. The fresher they are, the better they'll taste.

BASIC CANNING PROCEDURES

1. Gather together enough canning jars to handle your harvest. To make a rough estimate, fill one jar with beans of whatever sort

you are going to can, and measure the amount it holds. Basically, to get 1 pint of canned snap beans, you will need ⅔ pound of beans; for 1 pint of shell beans, you will need 2 quarts in the pod. Wash the jars and lids in hot, clean, soapy water. Or better yet, run them through the dishwasher, all cycles. Keep them hot. Check each rim and discard any that are chipped or cracked.

2. In a large pan, arrange the jar lids and pour boiling water over them. Or, run these through the dishwasher and don't open the dishwasher until the drying cycle is completed.

3. While you are working, store the picked beans in the refrigerator. Estimate the amount of beans you can process in one canned load, and, in cold water, wash that amount. Don't soak the beans—it leaches out some of the nutrition. When cleaning, *lift* the beans from the water. Don't pour them out, or you'll cover them with the dirt or sand you are trying to get rid of.

4. Prepare the beans as instructed in the recipes that follow. Sort them according to size and thickness. Blanch beans of the same size in the same lot so that they'll cook evenly.

5. Turn the clean, drained, sorted, and, if necessary, cut up beans into a wire basket or colander and set in a large kettle full of rapidly boiling water. Do not cover the kettle. Have the heat on high. Let the water return to a boil and time the blanching period from the moment it begins to boil again (see individual recipes for blanching times). Lift the beans from the kettle, but retain the water. Some of it will be used to fill the jars, and whatever is left can be used for the next batch.

6. If you have a wide-mouth funnel, place it over the canning jar and pour the beans through the funnel. If you don't have a wide-mouth funnel, spoon the beans quickly into the jar. Keep the jar threads clean.

Pack shell beans, limas, and garbanzos to within 1½ inches of the jar rim, and add boiling water to within 1 inch of the rim. Pack snap beans to within 1 inch of the jar rims and fill with boiling water, leaving ½ inch of headroom.

7. Air bubbles generally form in the liquid along the sides and near the rim top. Use a rubber spatula to rub them out. Wipe the jar threads and rims clean as a whistle; cap, and seal following instructions on pages 34–35.

8. Shortly before you are ready to fill the canner with jars, set

the canner over medium heat and set the rack on the bottom. If you are using a regular pressure cooker and have no rack, improvise with a small, round cooling rack for baked products. Add boiling water. For small canners and pressure cookers, water should be 1 inch deep; for large canners add water 2 inches deep. Or follow the recommendations that come with your canner.

As each jar is filled, cleaned, and capped, set it inside the canner to stay hot. When placing the jars in the canner, space them far enough apart so that steam can circulate all around each. Cover the canner and fasten the lid.

9. As soon as steam starts to whistle through the open petcock, start timing: Allow 7 to 8 minutes for the pressure to build, then close the petcock and start counting the processing time at that moment. The amount of pressure required is based on altitude. For each 1,000 feet above sea level, add ½ pound pressure to the processing time given in recipes.

10. As soon as the processing time is up, take the canner from the heat. Wait two minutes (or follow the manufacturer's instructions), then open the petcock. If no steam escapes, remove the cover; otherwise wait until steam is finished escaping. Use a jar lifter or a heavy oven mitt to remove the jars and set them, cap side up, on a rack to cool. Don't place the jars on a cold surface. If you don't have a rack, use towels. For the cooling period, choose a place away from cold drafts. Let jars cool for 12 hours.

11. When the jars are cool, test the seal according to the manufacturer's instructions. If the seal has failed on a jar, repack the jar and reprocess. Or refrigerate the beans, and use them within a day or so.

SEALING

Canned goods are vacuum-sealed by the processing. When a jar is closed at normal temperature, the air pressure within and without the jar is the same. As the jar is heated, everything in it expands (therefore we leave headroom, as you will see below), the air inside the jar is forced out, and the air pressure inside becomes less than that outside. As the jar cools, everything in it shrinks, a partial vacuum is formed, and atmospheric pressure of almost fifteen pounds per square inch, at sea level, holds the lid down and keeps the jar sealed. The sealing compound on Mason dome lids and the rubber of the rings used with zinc caps keeps the air from returning into the sealed jar. Naturally, the seal must be perfect if the foods inside are to be preserved.

To guarantee a good seal, make sure lids and jar rims are absolutely clean of foods. Make sure you leave headroom so foods can expand without pressuring the jar lid.

Be absolutely certain that jar rims have no hairline cracks. Run your finger over the rim of each jar before using. Follow the instructions for testing your jar seal after cooling the jars, with each jar each time you can. Once the seal is secure, you can remove the screw cap, wash it thoroughly, and store it.

Three ways to test the seal after processing in a pressure canner or a boiling-water-bath canner: You can hear a metallic snap as the lid becomes sealed while the jar is cooling; listen for it. Tap the lid with a spoon. A clear ringing sound means the jar is correctly sealed; when food is touching the lid, the sound will be dull. Feel the seal—press the center of the lid. If it is down and won't move, the jar is sealed. Tilt the jar to one side; if no food seeps out, the seal usually is perfect. If the jar is not sealed, reprocess the food. When the seal is assured, remove the screw band, wash it, and store for use the next time.

Altitude affects the number of pounds of pressure at which you pressure can. In boiling-water-bath processing, it affects the length of time you process the foods in the bath. The pressure poundages and boiling-water-bath processing-time periods for the recipes in this book are for specific altitudes. If you live at higher altitudes, refer to the Altitude Charts (pages 36–37) to adjust either the pressure poundage or the time of processing, depending on which method is called for.

CANNING SNAP AND OTHER EDIBLE-PODDED BEANS

Harvest young beans between 6 to 8 inches long, just before you are ready to can. Big fat older beans may be canned, too, but these must be French-cut. Whole young beans, with the ends trimmed off, aligned in symmetrical bunches, look truly elegant in a can.

Review the basic canning steps just described and proceed as follows:

1. Wash the beans in several changes of cold water.

2. Lay beans of similar size and thickness in rows on a cutting board and slice off top and bottoms. Or, snip tops and bottoms from fat beans and cut into 2-inch pieces. French-cut very thick beans (slice them down the middle, but not down the seam).

3. Bring a 6-quart kettle containing 4 quarts of water to a rapid boil and drop the beans into the water. When the water returns to a boil, count out 3 minutes, then remove the beans from the water. Reserve the water and bring it back to a boil.

Pack the beans at once into hot clean jars, leaving 1 inch of headroom between the beans and the jar rim. Add ½ teaspoon of salt to each pint jar, or 1 teaspoon to each quart jar. Cover with the boiling blanching liquid, leaving ½ inch of headroom.

4. Follow steps 7 through 11 in Basic Canning Procedures (pages 33–34). At sea level process pints for 20 minutes and quarts for 25 minutes at 10 pounds pressure in pressure canners. Process pints 40 to 45 minutes in ordinary pressure cookers. Add ½ pound pressure for each 1,000 feet of altitude above sea level.

CANNING FRESH LIMAS AND OTHER SHELL BEANS

Harvest the beans shortly before canning and be aware that you'll have to invest time in shelling lima and soybeans. Wash the pods

PRESSURE-CANNING ALTITUDE CHART

ALTITUDE ABOVE SEA LEVEL	PROCESS RECIPES AT:
2,000 to 3,000 feet	11½ pounds
3,000 to 4,000 feet	12 pounds
4,000 to 5,000 feet	12½ pounds
5,000 to 6,000 feet	13 pounds
6,000 to 7,000 feet	13½ pounds
7,000 to 8,000 feet	14 pounds
8,000 to 9,000 feet	14½ pounds
9,000 to 10,000 feet	15 pounds

BOILING-WATER-BATH ALTITUDE CHART

IF ALTITUDE IS OVER:	ADD TO PROCESSING TIMES 20 MINUTES OR LESS	ADD TO PROCESSING TIMES OVER 20 MINUTES
1,000 feet	1 minute	2 minutes
2,000 feet	2 minutes	4 minutes
3,000 feet	3 minutes	6 minutes
4,000 feet	4 minutes	8 minutes
5,000 feet	5 minutes	10 minutes
6,000 feet	6 minutes	12 minutes
7,000 feet	7 minutes	14 minutes
8,000 feet	8 minutes	16 minutes
9,000 feet	9 minutes	18 minutes
10,000 feet	10 minutes	20 minutes

thoroughly and drain them. If the pods are really tough, plunge them for 1 minute into boiling water, cool them in cold water in the sink, then pull the string tip down hard. Or use a sharp knife or a sharp scissors to snip them open down one side. Shell the beans.

Review the eleven canning steps described previously and then follow these instructions:

1. Sort the beans, if it seems necessary, into small, medium, and large sizes, and boil beans of similar size together.

2. Bring a large kettle full of water to a rapid boil, and drop the beans into the water. When the water returns to a boil, count 3 minutes. Drain, reserve the water, and bring it back to a boil. Pack the beans at once into hot clean jars, leaving 1½ inches of headroom between the beans and the jar rim. Add ½ teaspoon of salt to each pint, 1 teaspoon to each quart. Cover with boiling blanching liquid, leaving 1 inch of headroom.

3. Follow steps 7 through 11 in Basic Canning Procedures (pages 33–34). At sea level process pints for 40 minutes and quarts for 50 minutes at 10 pounds pressure. If the beans are large, process 10 minutes longer for both pints and quarts. Add ½ pound pressure for each 1,000 feet of altitude above sea level.

CANNING SUCCOTASH

Succotash is a mixture of lima beans (or shell beans of another sort—but not reds) and corn kernels, using 10 cups of beans for every 20 ears of corn.

Review the basic canning steps described on pages 32–34 and proceed as follows:

1. Husk, remove the silk, and wash the corn. Cover with boiling water and boil for 5 minutes. Remove the corn, reserving the water. Hold the cobs upright and with a sharp knife, cut the kernels cleanly from the cobs. Don't scrape the cobs. For each cup of limas or fresh shell beans prepare and measure out ⅔ cup of corn kernels.

2. Bring the water the corn boiled in back to a boil and set the measured limas or shell beans into it. If necessary, add more boiling water to bring the water to a level back up to cover the beans. When the water starts to boil again, start counting 3 minutes.

3. Remove the beans from the water, combine corn and beans in a large bowl, then pack into hot clean jars. Leave 1½ inches headroom. Bring the cooking water back to a boil and pour over the jars leaving 1 inch of headroom. Add ½ teaspoon of salt for each pint jar and 1 teaspoon for each quart jar.

4. Follow steps 7 through 11 in Basic Canning Procedures (pages 33–34). At sea level process pint jars for 1 hour and quart jars for 1 hour and 25 minutes at 10 pounds pressure. Add 1 pound pressure for each 1,000 feet of altitude above sea level.

5

Beans in the Cooker

There are three ways to cook shell beans, fresh or dry, but in my opinion only one basic way to cook snap beans when they're from your own garden. We should not even discuss tough, thick, fat, old, ugly, and limp snap beans that someone sold to you. They shouldn't have sold beans like that and you shouldn't have bought them. However, if you do get stuck with such beans, French-cut them (slice them down the middle, but not down the seam) and then follow directions below for cooking fresh snap beans.

COOKING SNAP BEANS

To get the best flavor and color from fresh green beans, set a big kettle of water to boil, pick pencil-slim beans about 6 to 7 inches long from the garden, snip off the ends as quickly as you can, and toss them a few at a time into the water. Don't add salt, and don't cover the pot.

Try to keep the water boiling rapidly all the time the beans are being added. (A large kettle will enable you to do this.)

Cook the beans just until the color begins to change. When you first put them in, they'll turn a deeper green. In 7 to 10 minutes, when a few beans show signs of turning from this deep green to a yellower green, test the beans. If they're just about tender, drain them quickly in a colander and return the pot to the heat while they're draining. Then return the beans to the pot, shake the beans over the heat till the moisture is gone, then butter them, add salt to taste, turn off the heat, partially cover, and serve as soon as you can.

If a few of the beans picked were large, French-cut them so they'll be the same thickness as the rest.

Yellow or wax beans don't have to be cooked on quite such a hysterical note to be perfect. Pick the beans when the color has changed from green-yellow to a strong yellow but before the beans inside the pods begin to get big and lumpy. Pick them just before cooking. Snip off the ends. If they're very long and large, cut them into 1- or 2-inch pieces. Put them a few at a time into a lot of boiling water.

The water doesn't have to be kept boiling every minute.

Cover the beans, and when they are just about tender, in about 12 to 15 minutes, drain the water and return the beans to the saucepan. Shake them over heat to dry the moisture, then add whole milk (a dash of half and half with it is nice) and salt and pepper to taste. Add just enough milk—½ cup or so—so that you can see it in the bottom of the pot through the beans. Bring the milk to a simmer and let the beans finish tenderizing in the milk, stirring occasionally—4 or 5 minutes. The milk will reduce and become creamy by the time the beans are completely done.

COOKING SHELL BEANS

To add to the other confusions surrounding shell beans, cooking times for these, whether fresh or dry, are hard to determine. Impossible, in fact. The amount of time necessary will vary considerably from one kind of bean to another: Fresh blackeyes and small limas cook rather quickly, while dark red kidneys and soybeans and small white beans cook very slowly. Cooking time also differs from one seedsman's variety to another, according to the season during which they were grown, and according to your region. If there was lots of rain, fresh shell beans are usually quicker to cook; if it was a dry year, they may take more time.

When we get down to the dry shell beans, variables in cooking times are further complicated by the age of the beans. And you can't really tell from looking at a dry bean how old it is. You simply have to test the beans for tenderness.

FRESH SHELL BEANS IN A SAUCEPAN

Cooked in a saucepan on top of the stove, fresh baby limas should take 20 to 30 minutes, depending on size. They may take more, but they probably won't take less. Have the water boiling before you put them in. Cover the pot. Bring the water back to a boil, then reduce the heat and simmer them until they are tender. Drain the beans, return to the pot, toss them in the pot over medium heat to evaporate the moisture, then butter the beans and add salt and pepper to taste.

Other fresh shell beans are cooked the same way but will probably take longer—up to an hour. The only way to be sure is to check as they cook. Some will take even more than an hour.

TO SOAK OR NOT TO SOAK

Efforts are being made to process commercial dry beans so that they'll cook more quickly. However, I can't say that all the beans on the market at this time are processed for quick cooking. Most are not. Growers are keen to tell us that their beans cook quickly.

Some packages say there's no need to soak. Others say all dry beans should be soaked. Since beans that should be soaked and aren't can take forever to cook, I soak all dry beans except those intended for the slow cooker, or for slow-cooking stews and soups.

The California Dry Bean Advisory Board found after extensive testing that beans cooked in a slow cooker do not need soaking first. Recently, that information has been modified, as noted below.

There are lots of ways to soak beans, some dating back to grandmother's day. Discouraged today by most authorities is the addition of baking soda to the soaking or cooking water, although salt water does seem to render beans a bit more firm. The beans, however, taste just as flavorful if salted after cooking.

The two popular methods for soaking at the moment are the *overnight soak*, and the *quick boilup soak*. To overnight-soak dry shell beans, wash and pick over the beans, remove floaters, and put the beans in a pot with water to cover or with water three times the volume of the beans, and let soak overnight—or 10 to 12 hours. You may soak them longer if you like; it won't hurt.

The quick-soak method, favored by many nutritionists, is to cover the beans with three times their volume of water, bring to a rapid boil, remove from the heat, cover, and let stand for 1 hour. Then they are ready to cook. Occasionally a recipe calls for a 2-hour soak.

The soaking water, though it leaches relatively few nutrients, is considered precious by nutritionists, so don't throw it away. Use it to cook the beans.

DRY SHELL BEANS IN A SAUCEPAN

To cook the soaked beans in a saucepan, return them to the heat in the water in which they have soaked, turn the heat to high, cover, bring to a boil, reduce the heat, and simmer until they are tender.

You can expect soaked dry shell beans to require anywhere from 45 minutes to 3 hours to tenderize. Blackeyes might take as little as 45 minutes, while small whites and dark red kidneys may take as long as 3 hours, and soybeans, 2 to 4 hours.

Check the beans after the first half hour. If the water level is below the beans, add more water. Check several times more as the beans begin to tenderize to make sure they still have enough water. They swell, taking in water, as they cook to two or three times their dry volume, depending on kind. Most double in size, but soybeans often triple.

If the beans are to be eaten when just cooked, plain, I let the cooking water reduce to almost zero as the beans finish cooking. It seems to me they taste better—mealier—that way. However, if bean water will be needed to complete the recipe, add water as it evaporates and is absorbed.

Once the beans have finished cooking, I add salt, pepper, and butter to taste if they are to be served plain and keep them covered on the back of the stove until serving time.

FRESH SHELL BEANS IN A PRESSURE COOKER

A pressure cooker is definitely an aid in getting fresh shell beans to the table in a hurry. The fastest cooking of the fresh shell beans, in my experience, are the small lima beans. The slowest cooking are the fresh soybeans.

Small fresh limas in a pressure cooker take between 2 and 3 minutes depending on size. Fresh blackeyes may cook just as quickly. The relatively fresh green soybeans in a pressure cooker can take 1½ hours. The other beans take somewhere between those two cooking times—maybe 20 to 30 minutes. In the instructions that come with your pressure cooker check the water needed and the timing required for fresh shell beans. If they're overcooked, fresh shell beans turn mushy and lose their taste.

DRY SHELL BEANS IN A PRESSURE COOKER

Consult your pressure cooker's instructions for water and timing on dry shell beans. Soak the beans as described on pages 41–42. Don't fill the cooker more than ⅓ full of dry beans and water—beans expand and may clog the vent. If your cooker's instructions don't discuss dry beans, measure the beans and add three times as much water. Start checking for tenderness at 40 to 50 minutes. Here again I can't give specific cooking times.

DRY SHELL BEANS IN A SLOW COOKER

For dry beans slow cookers are wonderful. Doris Hebert, of the California Dry Bean Advisory Board, has probably cooked more dry shell beans than most of us, and she says that when she puts the beans—with or without other ingredients—into the cooker at 7:30 in the morning, they are invariably cooked and just right by the time she gets home after work 10 to 12 hours later.

After a lot of testing in their kitchens, the California Dry Bean Advisory Board advised against soaking dry shell beans (excluding small whites) before cooking in a slow cooker. (I suggest that dark red kidneys, too, be excluded from that recommendation.)

To cook beans in a slow cooker, wash and pick them over, then place the beans with three times their volume of water in the slow cooker, cover, and cook till tender. Cook the beans on the low heat setting 10 to 12 hours. Blackeye beans probably cook more quickly. If using the high-heat setting, 5 or 6 hours is enough.

The great advantage in cooking dry shell beans in a slow cooker is that you don't have to keep checking to see if the water is gone. A slow cooker lets very little steam escape on the high setting and none on low, so the beans are never in danger of burning.

SPROUTING BEAN SEEDS

Soybeans as well as any viable (live) bean seed can be turned into a bean sprout. The only caution: For sprouting buy untreated, chemical-free seeds. Health food stores are a good place to find them, and Walnut Acres, Penns Creek, Pennsylvania 17862, is a good mail-order source. One of the great advantages in using fresh sprouts rather than the dry beans is that in the sprouting process, the gases and carbohydrates in the starchy seeds are transformed. The flavor—beany!

A bean sprout is a crisp, little beginning bean plant and it "sprouts" from a bean seed when the seed is kept moist and warm for a period of time—one to three days, usually. You'll find recipes for sprouted bean seeds on pages 53–57.

Bean sprouting is simple: Soak the beans overnight, drain them, keep them moist for the next 3 to 5 days, then pick a crop of crisp edible little shoots. Makes a fun and economical mini-crop for the kitchen gardener in periods of cool weather when the garden is miserly or nonexistent.

Detailed instructions on handling and cooking sprouts appear in chapter 7, which is all about soybeans. As a rule of thumb, regular bean seeds yield about 3 cups of sprouts for every 1 cup of beans. Harvest them at ¼ to ½ inch long. After harvesting, refrigerate, covered, and they'll be fresh for about 3 days.

Bean sprouts can be used in salads, cooked in stews, strewn as a decorative bed or garnish for roasts and sliced meats, or blended in dips and purees. In other words, they're flexible and can be incorporated one way or another into any dish that will benefit from their nutritional properties. Before using sprouts in salads or dishes where they'll be eaten raw, parboil the beans for 5 minutes in rapidly boiling water or steam them for 10 to 15 minutes, or until they reach the degree of tenderness the dish requires.

HINTS AND TIPS

In the chapters that follow there are recipes for both snap and shell beans. These recipes come from all over the country and many reflect individual and regional approaches to similar themes. Before you start cooking, there are a number of useful things to remember.

DRY BEANS SWELL: For every cup of dry beans, you'll probably get 2 cups cooked, and with some beans 2½ or 3 cups cooked.

USE THREE TIMES AS MUCH WATER: If you are lacking exact cooking information, start with three times as much water as dry beans.

ADDING EXTRA WATER: Beans cooking on top of the stove in a saucepan, covered, will probably need 1 quart more of water added during the cooking period.

YOU LOSE LOTS OF WATER: Uncovered beans at a simmer can run out of water in just half an hour.

HOW MUCH BEAN LIQUID? It takes about ⅔ cup of bean cooking liquid to cover about 2 cups of cooked beans. It takes about ½ cup water to cover 1 cup dry shell beans.

INDIVIDUAL PORTIONS: Half to 1 cup cooked shell beans is considered one portion, or serving. It takes ¼ cup dry to make ½ cup cooked; ½ cup dry to make 1 cup cooked.

TESTING FOR DONENESS: To test for doneness, blow gently on a spoonful of cooked beans. When almost tender but not yet at the point where they will break up (very soft), the skins will break and peel back if you blow them.

ADDING ACIDS: Acids, such as vinegar and those found in tomatoes, added to beans before they have become at least somewhat tender, may harden them and delay the cooking time. Therefore, most recipes—except for some that utilize slow cookers—recommend that beans be cooked to tenderness before they are combined with acid ingredients.

6

The Mighty Soybean

The mighty soybean is seen by some as the answer to everything—from rickets to plastic shortages. It comes from China, where it is credited with making the northern Chinese grow taller than the southern Chinese. (Scandinavians are taller than southern Europeans, but I don't think they eat more soybeans.) In any case, there's little quibble about the food value and versatility of soybeans. They can be eaten as sprouts, as snap beans, as fresh shell beans (rather like limas), or dry. They are bland in flavor but excellent for combining with other foods.

First imported from China to the United States around the turn of the century, they got a real start here during the Second World War; and the big health food awareness of the swinging sixties upped their glamor considerably. During the war, emergency food commissions declared that of natural foods soybeans have the highest nutritive value for the storage space they require and offer the highest nutritive value for the least money. Because of their protein and fat content, soybeans have a remarkable power to satisfy hunger; and because of their calcium, iron, phosphorus, potassium, B vitamins, vitamins C (in the sprouts) and A, choline, biotin, and inositol, not to mention the famous bean proteins, they're tops on nutritionists' lists. Today America is a leading producer of soybeans for commercial use. Mung beans (see pages 48–49) are rich in choline, vitamin A, E, and C, and have a pealike flavor.

GROWING SOYBEANS

My first introduction to soybeans was in the form of sprouted beans, which I used for Chinese dishes. I am embarrassed to admit that I originally thought they came in two sizes—big sprouted beans and tiny sprouted beans. Now I know that the little green ones, the very fine sprouts, are sprouted mung beans, and the fat yellow kind are sprouted soybeans.

Soybeans and mung beans are grown the way common beans are grown in the garden. Thousands of varieties of soybeans have been introduced from the Orient, and they vary in length of growing time from 75 to 200 days. They differ a lot in shape, color, and quality. Some are suited only to specific climates and localities; for example, years ago New York State University developed the Seneca, which is ideal for areas frost-free from late May to mid-September. The mature bean is medium size and light yellow. Early varieties such as the Seneca are the best producers in northern regions. Local State Extension Services can recommend soybeans for your particular locality.

In Canada, early research showed that some varieties proved suitable for home gardens, notably Fuji Giant Green and Willomi, and their offspring. If you want to select from your favorite catalog, buy according to the length of your growing season. The beans are planted in mid-spring, when the soil is warm (when corn is planted and apple blossoms fall), and *must* mature before frost. Very early varieties take 100 days to mature, or somewhat less; early types take 100 to 110 days; medium-early types take 110 to 120 days. Mid-season varieties take 120 to 130 days; late mid-seasons, 130 to 140 days; late varieties take 140 to 160 days; and very late varieties take 160 days or more.

If you want to have soybeans to use fresh over a long period, plant varieties all at the same time, in spring, but with days to maturity spaced at 10- to 15-day intervals.

Soil for soybeans should, like soil for common beans, be well-worked, good garden loam, and rather rich. Soil good for corn is good for soybeans. Like common beans, soybeans fix nitrogen from the air in the soil. They have a better ability to do this, especially in poor soil, if inoculated with soybean bacteria. To inoculate and grow soybeans, treat them as other beans described in chapter 2.

Soybeans' major enemies are rabbits and, in some areas, grasshoppers. They seem to stand droughts better than regular beans but do poorly when there are lots of weeds. You can harvest soybeans for use when the beans are fully developed but *before* the pods turn yellow. Most varieties stay at this stage for a week or 10 days. The pods can be picked every 3 or 4 days, or the plants can be pulled up and the beans harvested later.

If you want soybeans to dry, let the pods mature on the vines. When the leaves have fallen and the pods are brown, pull the plants up and beat out the beans, as described in chapter 2.

SPROUTING SOY- AND MUNG BEANS

If soybean sprouts are what you're after, select a variety for growing that is recommended for sprouting. Or sprout mung beans, which seem a little easier. You can also sprout pintos, garbanzos, and other grains and seeds (see pages 44–45, chapter 5), but soybeans and mung beans are those most commonly used.

Varieties that have been recommended for sprouting in the past are the Cayuga, Seneca, and Ontario. Other standbys have been Richland, Chief, Illinois, Manchu, Wisconsin, Mount Carmel, Otooton, and Peking. Some feed-and-seed dealers handle beans for sprouting, and, of course, so do the health food stores and health food mail order suppliers. If you buy dry soybeans for sprouting, make sure that they are first-quality beans, fully matured but not more than a year old. If you grow your own for sprouting, use the beans before you plant next year's crop.

Beans will sprout at any season, but they may get moldy if they are sprouted during hot, humid weather. Soybeans, which sprout in 3 to 5 days, are the most "instant" of all vegetables. They need neither soil nor sunshine to grow and take only 10 to 20 minutes to cook. And the sprouted beans are higher in food value. Vitamin C is formed, and two of the B vitamins, niacin and riboflavin, increase in quantity. Sprouted beans are also a good source of calcium.

As to flavor, they taste crisp—and watery—and faintly beany, but mostly bland. They provide texture rather than flavor, but they are very good for nutrition; and as a stretcher they blend with almost anything from fish to beef.

The first step in sprouting is to wash and pick over the beans; discard broken pieces. Next, soak the beans overnight in enough lukewarm water to cover them—by measure, three or four times as much water as beans—and in the morning rinse them clear in cold water and discard floaters. The beans will double in size.

Drain: spread the beans out in wide-mouth containers that have drainage holes in the bottom, such as flower pots. (Plug the drainage holes with bits of damp sponge.) The sprouted beans swell to four or more times their original volume, so spread them out over the bottoms and give them lots of headroom. To gauge quantities, the rule of thumb is that 1 cup of soybeans yields 3 cups of sprouts. (One cup of mung beans yields more, about 4 cups of sprouts.)

Set the bean containers on their sides in a dark, warm place, but not warmer than 75 or 80 degrees Fahrenheit. The dark end of a kitchen counter might be a good place. Lay over the bean tops a clean paper towel wrung out in cold water.

Two or three times a day water the beans as follows: Fill the containers to overflowing with water, then drain completely. The first day use lukewarm water, the following days when the sprouting beans are generating heat, use cold water. If the sprouts get too warm, they'll spoil. If you find they are heating up, insert a thin roll of wire screen in the middle of the container to improve air circulation.

The sprouts will get to be 1 to 2 inches long in 3 to 5 days. The skins of the beans will be loose. Wash these away under cold running water. The remaining bean and the little stem constitute a bean sprout. Covered, sprouts will stay fresh in the refrigerator for about 3 to 4 days. Mung beans are sprouted the same way; but they are ready in 3 to 4 days, and sprouts are only ½ to 1 inch long.

SPROUTS IN SALADS

A handful of bean sprouts improves the nutritional value of any salad and adds texture to it as well. To prepare sprouts for use in salads, rinse the raw sprouts, parboil for 5 minutes in salted water, drain, and chill. Or steam small sprouts for 5 to 10 minutes over medium heat, big sprouts 15 minutes. Bean sprouts sold in cans have been parboiled already.

COOKING SOYBEANS

Soybeans can be cooked fresh or they may be dried. (see page 51 for instructions for cooking frozen soybeans.) Dried soybeans are of two sorts, yellow and green. The greens are fresher than the yellows and have the best flavor for cooked shell bean dishes. That's a prejudice, perhaps, but it is backed by a nutritionist-vegetarian acquaintance of mine. The yellows are often used for sprouting; in cooked shell bean dishes they take longer to cook.

The flavor of cooked fresh green soybeans is rather like limas, and the beans are a little more tender and flavorful than cooked dry, yellow soybeans.

One popular method for shelling the beans is to pour boiling water over them and let them stand for 5 minutes. Drain, then break the individual pods crosswise and squeeze the beans out. They're bigger than the tiny mung beans, and they're round. Though the flavor is reminiscent of limas, it's nuttier, and the beans are chewier. Be sure to try the recipe for Plain Fresh Soybeans on page 52.

A word of warning: Don't eat soybeans raw. They taste terrible, but even if you don't think so, before cooking, the beans (not the sprouts, however) contain an antienzyme factor that destroys the enzymes needed for digestion. That makes the raw beans virtually indigestible.

CANNING SOYBEANS

Fresh green soybeans can be canned if you follow the general instructions in chapter 4 for canning shell beans. Blanch them first for 3 minutes in lots of boiling water (see page 28). Some authorities recommend the addition of 1 teaspoon salt and ½ or 1 teaspoon granulated sugar for each 2 cups of raw soybeans. Pack them in 1-pint jars to within 1 inch of the jar top, add the sugar and salt, then fill to within ½ inch of the top with boiling liquid. Make sure the beans are just covered. Process in a pressure canner at 10 pounds pressure, sea level. Add ½ pound pressure for each additional 1,000 feet above sea level. For pint jars process 80 minutes, for quart jars 90 minutes.

You can also can cook soybeans that have been dried. Soak (pages 40–41); then use the soaking water to cook the beans till tender, and follow the general information just given for canning fresh soybeans.

FREEZING SOYBEANS

Before freezing fresh soybeans, check out the general instructions for freezing in chapter 3. Freezing soybeans, however, is a little special. Since the easiest way to shell the fresh beans is to boil the pods in water for a full 5 minutes, then to cool the pods quickly and squeeze out the beans, there is no need to blanch them first.

Wash and drain the beans after shelling to clear away pod debris, then pack as described in chapter 3, seal tightly, and freeze.

COOKING FROZEN SOYBEANS

You can cook frozen soybeans much the way you cook limas. For a cup of beans, set ½ cup of water boiling, put in the beans, and boil for 10 to 15 minutes, or until tender. Salt and season after cooking.

Cooked frozen soybeans can be used in recipes for baby limas that call for cooked or canned limas.

DRY SOYBEANS IN A PRESSURE COOKER

The long cooking period for dry soybeans can be tedious, but if you use a pressure cooker, the beans can be ready in about 1½ hours. For 2 cups of dry beans add 1½ cups water, soak for 2 hours as described on pages 40–41, and cook at 10 pounds pressure for 10 minutes.

SOYBEAN RECIPES

Plain Fresh Soybeans

This is a basic method for cooking the fresh hulled soybeans. The beans are flavored with butter and salt and pepper, but you can dress them any way you would dress limas (see chapter 8).

2 cups hulled fresh soybeans　*⅛ teaspoon black pepper*
1 cup boiling water　　　*2 to 3 tablespoons butter or*
¼ teaspoon salt　　　　　*margarine*

In a medium saucepan combine soybeans and boiling water; cover and cook until tender, about 12 to 30 minutes. Don't overcook or flavor will be lost. Even when cooked, the color will be bright green. Pour off liquid, return to heat, shake the saucepan to dry any remaining moisture, then toss beans with remaining ingredients and serve.

SERVES 4

Plain Dry Soybeans

Dry soybeans swell to two or three times their size when cooked, and they take a long time to cook, longer than most other beans—3 to 4 hours, sometimes.

1 cup dry soybeans　　*4 to 6 tablespoons butter or*
3 cups cold water　　　*margarine*
½ teaspoon salt

1. Wash and pick over the beans. Place in a large saucepan with the cold water, bring to a boil, remove from the heat, cover, and let stand 2 hours.
2. Return to the heat, bring to a rapid boil, cover, and simmer until tender, 3 to 4 hours usually. Check occasionally and add water if needed. Drain and add salt and butter or margarine.

SERVES 6 to 8

Roasted Soybeans

Another thought about the mighty bean, which, as stated before, isn't really a bean: Treat it as a peanut—roasted soybeans are a great snack.

1 cup dry soybeans	*3 cups fat for deep frying*
2 cups tepid water	*Salt to taste*

1. Soak the beans in the water until they are visibly swollen to twice their size (see pages 40–41 for soaking instructions). Dry the beans thoroughly on a paper towel.
2. Heat the fat to 350°F. and fry the beans, several at a time, 5 to 8 minutes, or until lightly browned and crisp. Drain on a paper towel and sprinkle with salt to taste.

YIELDS 1½ to 2 cups

Bean Sprout Salad

Parboil the sprouts as described on page 45. This salad is nice as a side dish served with Oriental meals.

2 cups chilled, parboiled bean sprouts (page 50)	*4 tablespoons soy sauce*
	1 tablespoon cold water
½ clove garlic, peeled and crushed	*½ teaspoon granulated sugar*
	½ teaspoon mild vinegar

1. Place the bean sprouts in a large bowl.
2. In a cup, combine the remaining ingredients, stirring until the sugar is dissolved, and mix with the bean sprouts.

SERVES 4

Bean Sprout Combination Salad

For this one use almost any bit of leftover cooked and chilled vegetable, except for bland ones like potatoes. Parboil the sprouts first (see page 45).

1 cup chilled, parboiled bean   SALAD DRESSING
  sprouts (page 50)   4 teaspoons soy sauce
1 cup cooked diced beets   1 teaspoon granulated sugar
1 cup shredded raw carrot   Lettuce leaves
1 cup shredded, seeded green   8 tablespoons minced parsley
  pepper
1 small yellow onion, peeled and
  minced

Combine the vegetables in a large bowl and toss with the dressing, soy sauce and sugar. Spoon into a salad bowl lined with lettuce leaves and sprinkle with parsley. Toss again before serving.

SERVES 6 to 8

Bean Sprout and Green Pepper Salad

Parboil the chilled sprouts according to the directions on page 50.

2 cups chilled, parboiled bean   ½ cup finely chopped yellow
  sprouts   onion
1½ teaspoon salt   1 large green pepper, seeded and
⅛ teaspoon black pepper   chopped
¼ cup vegetable oil   1 small head iceberg lettuce,
2 tablespoons mild vinegar   chopped

1. Place the sprouts in a large bowl.
2. In a cup combine the dressing ingredients and pour over the sprouts. Add onion, green pepper, and lettuce; toss to mix well.

SERVES 6 to 8

Bean Sprout and Carrot Slaw

Parboil the chilled sprouts according to the directions on page 50.

⅔ cup seedless raisins
  Boiling water to cover raisins
2 cups coarsely grated raw
  carrots
1 cup chilled, parboiled bean
  sprouts

⅔ cup mayonnaise
1 small yellow onion, peeled
1 teaspoon lemon juice
½ teaspoon soy sauce
¼ teaspoon salt

1. Measure the raisins and pour boiling water over them to cover. Let stand 10 minutes. When the raisins have plumped drain and dry them on a paper towel.
2. Combine the carrots and sprouts in a large bowl and add enough mayonnaise to moisten them. Grate the onion over the top, and add lemon juice, soy sauce, and salt. Toss to combine; add raisins and toss once more. Chill.

SERVES 6 to 8

Boston Baked Soybeans

You can use cooked, fresh, or dry soybeans as a substitute in recipes that ordinarily call for baby limas or small white beans. Boston Baked Beans (page 111), for instance, is very good with soybeans.

3 cups cooked or canned
  soybeans
1½ cups soybean cooking liquid
  Boiling water
¼ cup firmly packed light
  brown sugar

¼ cup light molasses
2 tablespoons cider vinegar
1 teaspoon salt
½ teaspoon black pepper
½ teaspoon dry mustard
¼ pound diced salt pork

Measure out the soybean liquid to make 1½ cups. If there's not enough, add boiling water. Combine everything but the salt pork in a small bean pot or a 1½-quart casserole. Place the salt pork squares on the beans and poke them down into it. Bake at 350°F. for about 2 hours. Check occasionally and add water if the dish is drying out.

SERVES 4 to 6

Soybean Cream Sauce

This cream sauce is more nutritious than one made with plain milk.

2 tablespoons butter or　　　　　*Pinch of ground nutmeg*
　　margarine　　　　　　　　*⅛ teaspoon black pepper*
2 tablespoons all-purpose flour　*1 cup hot Soybean Milk*
½ teaspoon salt　　　　　　　　*(pages 59–60)*

In a small saucepan over low heat melt the butter or margarine and stir in the flour to make a smooth paste. Add the seasonings; then stir in the Soybean Milk. Continue to stir until the sauce has thickened.

YIELDS 1 cup medium-thick sauce

Bean Sprout Suey

A number of classical Chinese vegetable recipes, such as this one, call for bean sprouts. I have found I can use bean sprouts as a substitute for almost any vegetable in a Chinese dish. If I use bean sprouts instead of snow peas, the flavor won't be the same, but the taste will be just as good.

This is a very fast dish to make and a favorite with my family and friends. It can be made with strips of any meat—preferably meat cooked only to a tender pink—or with chicken. Slicing the ingredients takes about 15 minutes—the cooking not much more than 10. You need a wok or a big iron skillet, very hot, for the results to be just right. Line up the ingredients, all cut and measured, by the wok or skillet, and work quickly.

2 tablespoons vegetable oil
1 medium yellow onion, peeled
    and cut into strips
1 large clove garlic, peeled
    and minced
4 medium stalks celery, cut in
    thin 4-inch long strips
1 cup green pepper, seeded and
    cut into thin strips
1 cup bean sprouts

½ pound fresh mushrooms, wiped
    clean and sliced thin
3 tablespoons butter, vegetable
    oil, or gravy drippings
1 to 2 cups cooked meat (page
    56), cut into thin strips
3 to 4 tablespoons soy sauce
1 tablespoon cornstarch
¼ cup cold water
3 cups hot cooked white rice

1. Set a wok or a large heavy skillet over high heat for 30 seconds or until it is sizzling hot. Add the oil and allow it to heat for about 20 seconds. Add the onion and garlic and sauté 1 minute, stirring constantly. Add the celery and sauté 1 to 2 minutes, stirring until the green color brightens. Add the pepper and cook 1 minute, stirring constantly. Add the bean sprouts and stir-fry for 1 minute. Make space in the center of the wok and add the mushrooms; stir a minute, then add the butter, oil, or drippings and stir 2 minutes more. Keep all ingredients moving in the wok or they'll burn. Push the mushrooms to one side and add the meat strips; stir until heated, 1 minute. Sprinkle with soy sauce and mix ingredients well. Then push to one side.

2. In a cup, mix cornstarch with water; pour into the wok and stir. Then mix in all the ingredients. When the ingredients are coated with a clear thick sauce—after about 2 more minutes of stirring—serve at once with hot white rice on the side.

SERVES 6

Haddock and Bean Curd

Prepare and measure all the ingredients and have them ready near the stove before you begin.

2 *tablespoons vegetable oil*	1 *scallion, peeled and cut into*
1 *pound fresh firm haddock,*	*1-inch lengths*
cut into 1-inch cubes	½ *cup water*
2 *tablespoons dry sherry*	1 *teaspoon salt*
2 *tablespoons soy sauce*	1 *cup Soybean Curd (page 59),*
1 *teaspoon minced fresh ginger or*	*cut into 1½-inch cubes*
½ *teaspoon ground ginger*	

Set a wok or a large heavy skillet over high heat and heat to sizzling. Swirl in the oil, reduce the heat to medium, add the fish chunks and sauté 3 minutes, stirring constantly, until they are brown on all sides. Add the sherry, soy sauce, ginger, scallion, water, and salt and simmer 1 minute more, stirring. Stir in the Soybean Curd. Simmer 4 minutes more, then serve at once.

SERVES 4

Bean Curd and Tomato Sauce

Healthy and different—tastes good, too.

¼ *cup vegetable oil*	2 *whole cloves*
1 *large yellow onion, peeled and*	⅛ *teaspoon black pepper*
sliced thin	1 *tablespoon cornstarch*
1 *large seeded green pepper,*	6 *tablespoons cold water*
cut into strips	4 *to 6 tablespoons butter or*
1 *small bay leaf*	*margarine*
1 *16-ounce can tomato sauce*	2 *cups Soybean Curd (page 59),*
2 *teaspoons salt*	*cut into ½-inch-thick slices*
1 *teaspoon granulated sugar*	

1. Heat the oil in a medium skillet over medium heat, and sauté the onion 3 minutes, then add the green pepper, and sauté 3

minutes more. Add next six ingredients; cook, stirring until the sauce is slightly thickened. In a cup mix cornstarch with water; pour into the skillet and stir and simmer until the sauce has thickened. Set aside.

2. Melt the butter or margarine in a medium saucepan over medium heat and sauté the Soybean Curd, stirring gently, until a light brown crust has formed. Serve Soybean Curd with the tomato sauce.

SERVES 6

Soybean Curd: Tofu

From Soybean Milk one can make soybean curd—that cheeselike, very bland white curd used in Chinese cooking. You need a thermometer for this.

1 quart Soybean Milk (pages 59–60)   *½ cup white vinegar*
¼ teaspoon salt

In a saucepan over medium heat, heat the Soybean Milk to 180°F., remove from the heat, stir in the vinegar, and set aside until a curd forms, 15 to 20 minutes. Line a colander with a double thickness of cheesecloth, and turn the curdled milk into it. Lift the cheesecloth and squeeze gently to drain away all the liquid. Fill the sink with cold water and dip the bag into the water several times to wash off excess acid. Return to the colander, and let drain for 1 hour. Then press to remove the remaining liquid. Mix in salt, pack into a 1-quart mold rinsed in water, cover, and store in the refrigerator until firm enough to cut.

YIELDS about 2 cups

Soybean Milk

Soybean milk is given to infants who can't handle cow's milk. The flavor is bland, almost tasteless, but the milk is a valuable source of protein. You can use it for making milk shakes, sauces, soups, custards, beverages, and sometimes in place of milk in baked goods (see recipes that follow). Use the pulp as a meat extender.

1 cup dry soybeans
6 cups water to cover beans
  Salt

1 teaspoon honey or light corn
  syrup

1. Wash and pick over the beans, cover them with the water in a medium saucepan, and soak them overnight (see pages 41–42).

2. In the morning rub the beans together with your hands, in the water, to remove the skins. Discard the skins, drain the beans reserving the water, and put the beans through the grinder using the fine blade, or through a food mill. Measure the liquid and add more water if needed to make 6 cups.

3. Place the ground beans and water in a saucepan, and bring to a boil. Simmer, uncovered, for 15 to 20 minutes, stirring. Strain through a double thickness of cheesecloth, and stir in ⅛ teaspoon salt and the honey or corn syrup into the milk. Refrigerate. Add ¾ teaspoon salt to the mash and moisten with a little Soybean Milk. Cover and refrigerate.

YIELDS about 1 quart of milk and 3 cups mash

Soybean Milk Shake

1 cup cold Soybean Milk
  (pages 59–60)
1 tablespoon clover honey or
  marmalade

¼ teaspoon vanilla
1 very large ripe banana
½ canned apricot
6 large ice cubes

Place all ingredients in the blender and turn to high. Blend until the shake is thick and the fruits are pureed—about 2 or 3 minutes.

SERVES 2

Soybean Milk Toddy

This is a nice warm drink for cold nights.

1 cup Soybean Milk (pages 59–60)
2 tablespoons honey
¼ teaspoon ground ginger

⅛ teaspoon ground nutmeg
⅛ teaspoon salt
½ teaspoon butter or margarine

Combine the ingredients in a small saucepan and heat, stirring till butter or margarine is melted.

SERVES 1

Soybean Pulp in Meat Patties

Soybean pulp is a great meat stretcher. One way to make pulp is to cook the beans—fresh, frozen, or dry—then put them through a food grinder using the fine blade, or a food mill.

½ pound ground beef	*¼ teaspoon black pepper*
1 cup cooked soybean pulp	*1 small yellow onion, peeled*
(see above)	*and grated*
2 teaspoons salt	*½ teaspoon garlic powder*

1. Place the ground beef in a medium bowl, stir in the soybean pulp, salt, pepper, and onion. Form into four thick patties.
2. Heat a heavy skillet to sizzling hot and sprinkle with more salt. Put in the patties and sprinkle with half the garlic powder. When the patties are well browned on the underside, turn and press hard with a spatula two or three times to flatten. Sprinkle with remaining garlic powder and cook another 3 or 4 minutes. Then turn off the heat and let them sit for a few minutes to finish cooking.

SERVES 4

FLOUR, FLAKES, AND GRITS

Making your own soybean flour is a bother, but lots of health food people do buy and use it regularly. The flour contains no gluten-forming proteins, so baked goods made with soybean flour alone won't rise. For baking, combine soybean flour with an equal amount of wheat flour. Or, think of it this way: You can substitute soybean flour for up to half the amount of any regular flour called for in a baking recipe, including cakes.

If you want to make Soybean Curd or *Tofu* (page 59), and don't want to bother with the grinding of the beans, buy flour and make it from that.

By grinding soybeans coarsely you can make soybean grits and soybean flakes. Grits have a texture similar to corn meal, while flakes look more like rolled oats. A friend of mine uses grits instead of meat in meatless dishes—she's a vegetarian—and in soups to thicken them, and she recommends them as a meat extender. The grits expand to double or triple their original volume when moistened.

7

Green Beans and Yellow Wax Beans

Green beans are one of the most popular home garden vegetables. Wax beans are very good, too. Though these beans taste best when they've just been picked, they can be stored in the refrigerator for up to two weeks. To prepare them for cooking, we used to have to yank away a seam string, but today the strings have been bred out of most home garden and commercial varieties, so all you have to do to prepare them for cooking is snip off the ends and wash the beans in cold water.

Hot cooked or canned beans combine well with hot cooked or canned carrots, celery, peas, onions, or limas, or other shell beans. They're great in a cream sauce to which a little mustard, horse-radish (try grated fresh horseradish and cream), or minced parsley has been added. Cream sauce flavored with nutmeg is especially nice.

Green beans cooked with dill seed, dill weed, or fresh dill is a favorite of mine, along with wax beans cooked in cream. For the basic cooking of fresh string beans, see chapter 5.

Cold cooked or canned beans are great in salads, especially if there is a little minced onion in the dressing. They taste best when they are combined with the salad dressing or a marinade dressing while they are still warm from cooking.

If you are buying rather than growing beans, consider 1 pound a fair amount for four people. If you are picking beans, one handful should be enough for each portion.

Kentucky Wonder Appetizer

Kentucky Wonders are one of the shell bean varieties that can be picked in the snap bean stage. They have a special flavor that some cooks think resembles that of okra.

4 cups Kentucky Wonder or other edible-pod shell beans	¼ cup mayonnaise
3 quarts rapidly boiling water	1 tablespoon curry powder
½ teaspoon salt	1 tablespoon lime juice, strained
1 cup sour cream	Salt to taste

1. Snip the stem ends from the beans but leave the pointed tips on. Drop the beans into the rapidly boiling water a few at a time; add more only when the water returns to a boil. Boil quickly, uncovered, until the beans are tender but still firm. Drain, and shake the beans in the pan over heat to remove remaining moisture. Salt lightly and chill.
2. Stir the remaining ingredients together to make a sauce. Chill.
3. Arrange the beans, pointed tips outward, on a plate with a bowl of sauce in the center and serve.

SERVES 6 to 10

Green Bean and Bagna Cauda Appetizer

This is a good way to serve those green beans you didn't pick quite soon enough. *Bagna cauda* means "hot bath."

2 to 3 cups green beans	½ pound butter or margarine
6 cloves garlic, peeled	1 cup olive oil
12 anchovy fillets in oil	Black pepper to taste

1. Prepare and cook the beans as for Dilled Green Beans (page 66), but omit the dill. Remove them from the water before they are quite tender. They should be a little crisp, not so wilted they can't stand straight. Chill.

2. Mash the garlic and anchovies in a wooden bowl or a mortar. Turn into a fondue pot and heat, stirring, until the mixture thickens. Stir in the butter or margarine, oil, and pepper. Cook for 3 minutes, then turn the flame to the lowest heat. Serve as hot dip for chilled beans.

SERVES 6 to 8

Green Bean Chowder

This takes a little time. It's a perfect illustration of the rather exquisite ways the French have with food.

1½ pounds green beans
2 to 3 quarts rapidly boiling
    water
3 tablespoons butter
2 cups beef consommé

2 medium potatoes, peeled and
    diced
Hot whole milk
Salt and pepper to taste

1. Wash the beans in cold water, snip off the stems and tips, and drop a few at a time into rapidly boiling water. Do not add more beans until the water returns to a boil. Cook, uncovered, just until a hint of yellow color appears on the beans, then drain. Return to the heat, add 2 tablespoons of the butter, and let simmer, uncovered, another few minutes.

2. Add the beef consommé and the diced potatoes and simmer until the potatoes are done (about 15 to 20 minutes). Place a little of the mixture at a time in the blender and blend at low speed until smooth. Return to the heat and add about ¾ to 1 cup hot milk to thin the chowder to the consistency of heavy cream. Heat through; season with salt and pepper to taste, and add the rest of the butter before serving hot.

SERVES 6

Dilled Green Beans

1 pound fresh green beans   *¼ to ½ teaspoon salt*
2 to 3 quarts rapidly boiling water   *2 tablespoons butter or*
1 big sprig fresh dill or ½ tea-   *margarine*
*   spoon dry dill weed or dill seed*

1. Drop the beans a few at a time into the rapidly boiling water with the dill; add more beans as the water returns to a boil. Boil, uncovered, 7 to 10 minutes, just until a hint of yellow color appears. Drain, return to the heat, shake the saucepan to remove any remaining moisture, sprinkle with salt and add butter or margarine, and toss the beans until the butter is melted.
2. If you used fresh dill, serve the beans with the wilted dill sprig on top.

SERVES 4

Green Beans Amandine

This is a classic way to prepare fresh green beans. It does a lot for frozen beans, too.

1 pound fresh or frozen green   *¼ cup blanched, slivered almonds*
*   beans*   *Salt to taste*
¼ cup butter

1. Prepare the beans and cook them as for Dilled Green Beans (page 66), but omit the dill. Keep them hot.
2. Melt the butter in a small saucepan over medium heat, and add the almonds. Stir over lowered heat until the almonds are lightly browned. Add salt.
3. Combine beans and almonds and serve at once.

SERVES 4

Green Beans in Anchovy Sauce

An Italian approach to beans—and very tasty.

1 pound green beans   *¼ teaspoon onion juice**
¼ cup butter or olive oil   *¼ teaspoon lemon juice*
1 teaspoon anchovy paste

1. Prepare the beans and cook them as for Dilled Green Beans (page 66), but omit the dill. Keep them hot.
2. Cream the butter in a small round bottom bowl, or place the oil in the bowl. Add remaining ingredients and mix until smooth. Add to beans and toss until beans are completely coated.

SERVES 4

* Obtain by pressing diced onion through a garlic press.

Green Beans with Mushrooms

1 pound green beans   *Pinch of salt*
¼ pound fresh mushrooms   *Freshly ground black pepper*
¼ cup butter or margarine   *to taste*

1. Prepare the beans and cook them as for Dilled Green Beans (page 66), but omit the dill. Keep them hot.
2. Wipe the mushrooms clean and slice thin.
3. Melt the butter or margarine in a large saucepan over medium heat, and sauté the mushrooms 5 minutes, until limp. Sprinkle salt over the mushrooms and stir once more. Add the drained, hot beans to the saucepan, toss well with mushrooms and butter, and season with pepper.

SERVES 4

Beans, Lebanon Style

I suggest using green beans here, but yellow beans can be used if you add a bit of paprika to improve the color. Cook yellows a bit longer.

1 pound green beans, washed
    and cut into 1-inch pieces
1 tablespoon butter or margarine
1 teaspoon chopped parsley
½ teaspoon granulated sugar

Salt to taste
1 tablespoon all-purpose flour
2 tablespoons plain yogurt
2 to 3 tablespoons cold water

Place cut-up beans in a saucepan with butter or margarine, parsley, sugar, and salt. Cover tightly and cook slowly until tender, 25 to 30 minutes. Check periodically. If too dry, add a little water so the beans will not burn. When tender, sprinkle the flour over the beans, stir, add the yogurt and water. Stir to combine, then cover and simmer a few more minutes, or until a bit of creamy sauce coats the beans.

SERVES 4

Green Beans in Sherried Mushroom Sauce

This is a good party vegetable—nice fresh green beans in a glamorous sauce.

2 pounds fresh green beans
4 quarts rapidly boiling water
¼ teaspoon salt
2 tablespoons butter
1 small yellow onion, peeled
    and minced
1 small clove garlic, peeled and
    minced

½ pound mushrooms, wiped clean
    and sliced thin
2 tablespoons all-purpose flour
½ cup hot beef bouillon
½ cup whipping cream
⅛ cup dry sherry

1. Wash the beans, snip off the stems and tips, and drop a few at a time into rapidly boiling water. Add more beans only when the water has returned to a boil. Cook until just a hint of yellow color appears on the beans—7 to 10 minutes—then drain, return to the heat, shake the saucepan to remove any remaining moisture. Add salt.

2. Meanwhile, melt the butter in a medium saucepan and sauté the onion and garlic about 5 minutes, until the onion is translucent. Add the mushrooms, and sauté about 5 minutes more, until limp.

Remove the pan from the heat. Add the flour, stirring. Add the bouillon and cream, stirring quickly to smooth out the sauce. Return to the heat and simmer until the sauce thickens. Add the sherry, cook 2 minutes more, then pour over the beans, and let sit by the heat for a few minutes before serving.

SERVES 8

Green Beans Fukien

Have all the ingredients measured before you begin.

2 *tablespoons vegetable oil*	2½ *cups green beans, cut into*
1 *medium clove garlic, peeled*	*diagonal pieces 1½ to 2*
and minced	*inches long*
1 *pound ground pork*	1½ *cups boiling water*
2 *tablespoons soy sauce*	1 *tablespoon cornstarch*
¼ *teaspoon salt*	¼ *cup cold water*
6 *slivered water chestnuts or*	½ *head lettuce, shredded*
½ *cup minced celery*	

1. Heat the oil in a very large skillet or a wok over high heat until it is almost smoking. Add the garlic and swish it around quickly. Add the pork, break it into bits, stirring for 1 or 2 minutes, or until browned well. Add the soy sauce, salt, and water chestnuts or celery and continue to stir for 2 minutes.

2. Add the beans, stir in quickly with the other ingredients, then pour in the boiling water in a thin stream. Stir once more and cover. Bring the contents of the skillet to a simmer, then turn down the heat and simmer 4 minutes.

3. Mix the cornstarch with the cold water. Check the beans for tenderness. A minute before they are tender, stir the cornstarch into the liquid in the skillet, and keep stirring as the sauce thickens and clears. Check the beans for doneness, and if needed, cook another minute or so.

4. Place the shredded lettuce in a warm shallow bowl and turn the beans and pork onto it.

SERVES 4

Green Bean Casserole

When your snap beans are bigger than you like, try this casserole.

2 pounds green beans
8 medium yellow onions, peeled
    and chopped
2 green peppers, seeded and
    ·chopped

¼ teaspoon ground thyme
½ teaspoon salt
⅛ teaspoon black pepper
 4 tablespoons butter, melted
½ cup bread crumbs

1. Heat the oven to 350°F.
2. Wash the beans in cold water, snip off the stems and tips, and drain well.
3. In a buttered 2-quart casserole, layer ⅓ of the beans, top with ⅓ of the onions, ⅓ of the peppers and 1 tablespoon of the butter. Repeat layers, seasoning each with a little thyme, salt, and pepper. Cover and bake 1½ hours, or until the beans are tender.
4. In a small saucepan over medium heat sauté the bread crumbs in the remaining 1 tablespoon butter for 3 or 4 minutes. Sprinkle over the beans and brown a bit more under a hot broiler before serving.

SERVES 8

Yellow Beans in Cream

4 to 6 cups yellow beans
2 to 3 quarts rapidly boiling
    water
⅔ cup light cream or half-and-
    half

Salt and freshly ground black
    pepper to taste
2 to 3 tablespoons butter or
    margarine
Pinch of ground nutmeg

1. Wash the beans and snip off the ends. (Pull strings if there are any.) Drop a few at a time into rapidly boiling water. Cover and cook until almost tender, 12 to 15 minutes. Drain, return to the heat, and shake the saucepan to remove any remaining moisture.
2. Pour the cream or half-and-half over the beans and simmer, uncovered, until the beans are quite tender. Drain, reserving the

cream. Add salt and pepper. Serve the beans in individual dishes with a little cream in each. Dot with butter or margarine and add a dash of nutmeg.

SERVES 4 to 6

Yellow Beans, Madrid Style

This recipe works very well with French-cut green beans too.

1½ pounds yellow beans
3 to 4 quarts rapidly boiling
water

3 tablespoons olive oil
2 medium cloves garlic, peeled
1 teaspoon paprika

1. Wash the beans and snip off the stems and tips. (Remove strings if there are any.) Throw the beans a few at a time into the boiling water. Cook until tender, 10 to 15 minutes. Drain, return to the heat, shake the saucepan to remove any remaining moisture.
2. As the beans finish cooking, prepare the sauce: In a large skillet over medium-low heat, heat the oil and slice into it the garlic. Make the slices thin. Cook the garlic, stirring, until golden. Remove the pan from the heat, stir in the paprika, then toss the beans in this sauce, and serve very hot.

SERVES 6

Purée of Yellow Beans

When yellow beans don't get picked quite on time, try preparing them this way.

1 pound yellow beans
2 to 3 quarts rapidly boiling
water
½ teaspoon salt

¼ cup whipping cream
2 tablespoons butter
Freshly ground black pepper
to taste

1. Wash the beans and snip off the stems and tips. Place them in the boiling water, cover and cook until tender, about 15 minutes.

Drain, return to the heat, shake the saucepan to remove any remaining moisture. Toss again with the salt.

2. Put the beans through a food grinder or a food mill. Return to the pot and add whipping cream, butter, and black pepper. Reheat over a very low flame, stirring until well mixed.

SERVES 4

Bean Salad Vinaigrette

This recipe combines cooked green and yellow beans in a sharp dressing and makes a great appetizer or salad.

1 pound yellow beans	*2 tablespoons tarragon vinegar*
1 pound green beans	*1 tablespoon minced shallot*
4 to 5 quarts rapidly boiling	*1 tablespoon minced chives*
water	*1 tablespoon minced parsley*
1 clove garlic, peeled	*1 teaspoon salt*
and crushed	*½ teaspoon dry mustard*
½ cup olive oil	*Salt and black pepper to taste*
2 tablespoons wine vinegar	

1. Wash the beans, snip off the ends, throw the yellow beans a few at a time into the boiling water, and when they are all in and boiling rapidly, add the green beans. Cook until the beans are just tender. Drain, return the beans to the heat, shake the saucepan to remove any remaining moisture. Turn off the heat and leave the beans in the pot, half-covered.

2. Combine the remaining ingredients and pour over the hot beans. Toss well, then turn into a salad bowl and allow to cool at room temperature. Taste, add more salt if needed and pepper to taste, cover, and chill before serving.

SERVES 8

Beans with Pimientos

This is a good Spanish approach to beans, whether green or yellow.

1 pound green or yellow wax beans, cooked
4 pimientos, washed
3 tablespoons olive oil

3 medium cloves garlic, peeled and minced
1 teaspoon chopped parsley
Salt and black pepper to taste

1. Heat the oven to 350°F.
2. Cook the beans as described in Dilled Green Beans (page 66), but omit the dill.
3. Meanwhile, brush the whole pimientos with 2 teaspoons of the oil and bake them until the skins are dry but not burnt. Cut the pimientos open (wear oven mitts), remove the seeds and stem ends, and cut the flesh into strips.
4. Heat the remaining oil in a skillet over medium heat and stir in the garlic and parsley. Cook 2 or 3 minutes until the garlic turns golden; then stir in the pimiento strips and stir and cook 1 or 2 minutes more.
5. Combine the pimiento strips with the cooked hot beans. Season with salt and pepper.

SERVES 4

Snap Beans, Southern Style

When beans you are growing have really gotten big on the vine, this is one way to cook them that won't make you wish you had picked them while they were still tender.

2 pounds snap beans
Boiling water to cover beans
¼ pound salt pork

½ teaspoon granulated sugar
Salt and black pepper to taste

Wash the beans in cold water and snip off the stems and tips. (Remove strings if there are any.) Place in a large kettle and cover with rapidly boiling water. Add pork and sugar. Bring the water back to a boil, cover, reduce the heat, and simmer until beans are very tender and the water is almost gone, about 1 hour. Taste and add salt and pepper, if needed.

SERVES 8

8

Lima Beans

LIMAS, SMALL AND LARGE

Although lima beans are popular in the home garden, they aren't as widely grown as the snap bean. In the North we can harvest baby limas, but these are really a warm-country legume, and northerners are more familiar with them in their frozen or dry state.

Lima and Pimiento Dip (page 75) illustrates a unique use of mashed shell beans made with cooked or canned large limas. The flavorings are typical, and the dip is scooped up with corn chips or crackers. Cooked shell beans of all sorts make an inexpensive and handy base for dips and snacks when you're caught short.

Some recipes here call for small limas and others for large limas. The small limas don't seem to thicken soups and stews the way many of the other cooked beans do—pinks and pintos and small white beans, for instance. Therefore, the recipe for Limas and Vegetable Chowder (pages 81–82) calls for small limas and includes potatoes to thicken the soup. Lima Soup with Ham Bone (pages 82–83), however, uses large limas and has no other thickener.

The meat with which limas are combined most often is ham. However, one of my favorite bean dishes is Lima Beans and Leg of Lamb (pages 87–88), a variation on the way the French cook *gigot et flageolets* or *gigot et haricots*. (The *flageolet* is a dry bean that is green, and the *haricot* a dry beige or white bean.)

Of all the dry beans limas are those most used in vegetable casseroles. If you use whites as a substitute for limas, the flavor won't change drastically, but if you use pink, red, or black beans, the taste will be quite different.

I find that limas in salads fail to absorb the dressing; it seems to slide off their skins. Other beans are better salad makers, but I have included two lima salad recipes, Lima Bean and Garbanzo Salad (pages 169–170) and Limas in Little Caesar Dressing (pages 76–77).

I saved Lima Bean Fruitcake (pages 88–89) for the end. It's a little like applesauce cake or banana bread—a textured sweet that's fun to make.

Lima and Pimiento Dip

A creamy, tart dip to serve with potato chips, crackers, or corn chips. Make sure the cheese is at room temperature—really soft.

3 cups cooked or canned large limas, drained
½ cup mayonnaise
2 to 4 tablespoon wine vinegar
Dash of Tabasco sauce
1 8-ounce package cream cheese at room temperature
2 tablespoons prepared mustard
1 teaspoon dill weed
2 tablespoons minced yellow onion
1 medium clove garlic, peeled and crushed
1 teaspoon salt
⅛ teaspoon white pepper
1 can pimientos, drained

Mash the limas in a large flat-bottom bowl with a potato masher. Add the mayonnaise, vinegar, and Tabasco sauce and mix well. Then stir in the remaining ingredients except for the pimientos, and mix well. Add the pimientos last and mix them in gently.

YIELDS about 3½ cups

Limas and Deviled Ham Dip

A sharply flavored dip that can, if you wish, be heated and turned
into a hot dish. Just place the finished dip in a hot skillet and stir
over the heat until bubbling. Dijon mustard is a flavorful French
mustard, but any good prepared mustard is a suitable substitute.

*1½ cups cooked or canned large
　　lima beans, drained
　3 tablespoons mayonnaise
　1 tablespoon wine vinegar
　2 teaspoons Dijon mustard
　½ teaspoon paprika
　1 2¼-ounce can deviled ham*

*2 hardboiled eggs, peeled and
　　chopped
2 tablespoons chopped chives
½ teaspoon salt
⅛ teaspoon black pepper
Corn chips or tostados*

Place the limas in a large, flat-bottom bowl, and with a potato
masher mash them, but don't squash so much as to make a paste.
Stir in the remaining ingredients except the corn chips or tostados.
Taste and add more seasonings if desired. Serve with corn chips
or tostados.

YIELDS 2 cups

Limas in Little Caesar Dressing

Caesar dressing is a famous West Coast invention made with a raw
egg and the seasonings listed here. Little Caesar dressing substitutes
mayonnaise as the thickener, and no egg is used. Plain croutons
sautéed in butter with a little garlic salt can be used if commercial
garlic croutons aren't available.

*1 large clove garlic, peeled
1 teaspoon salt
¼ teaspoon black pepper
⅛ teaspoon oregano
2 tablespoons wine vinegar
1 tablespoon lemon juice,
　strained
½ cup vegetable oil*

*3 tablespoons mayonnaise
6 anchovies, mashed
3 cups cooked or canned large
　　lima beans, drained
Grated Parmesan
Romaine lettuce
½ cup hot garlic croutons*

1. Into a large salad bowl, slice the garlic, sprinkle with salt, and mash to make garlic salt. Add the pepper, oregano, vinegar, and lemon juice. Beat in the oil and stir in the mayonnaise and anchovies. Toss the limas in the dressing and chill until ready to serve.

2. Sprinkle mixture generously with Parmesan cheese and turn into individual beds of romaine lettuce. Sprinkle with hot croutons.

SERVES 6

Fresh Lima Beans

2 cups fresh baby lima beans, shelled*
Water to cover beans
¼ teaspoon salt

2 tablespoons butter or whipping cream
1 teaspoon minced pimiento
Black pepper to taste

Combine the limas and the water in a medium saucepan, bring to a boil, cover, lower the heat, and simmer until tender, about 30 minutes. Drain, return to the heat, and shake the saucepan to remove any remaining moisture. When all the water is gone, sprinkle with salt and toss with butter or cream and the pimiento. Add pepper and more salt (if needed).

SERVES 4

* To shell the beans, cut thin strips from the inner edges of the pods with scissors or a sharp knife, or snap the pods open. Remove the beans.

Dry Baby Limas

2 cups dry baby lima beans
6 cups cold water
½ teaspoon salt
4 tablespoons butter or whipping cream

1 teaspoon minced pimiento
Black pepper to taste

1. Combine the limas and water in a large saucepan, bring to a boil, boil 2 minutes, remove from the heat, cover, and let stand 1

hour. Return to a boil, lower the heat, cover, and simmer about 1½ hours, or until tender.

2. Drain the beans thoroughly, return to the pot, sprinkle with salt and toss with butter or cream and pimiento. Add pepper and more salt (if needed).

SERVES 8

Lima Bean Bake

A great side dish reminiscent of Boston baked beans. If, at the end, there's more liquid than you want, turn the liquid into a saucepan and bubble rapidly, stirring, on the stovetop until it has thickened.

2⅔ cups (1 pound) dry large lima beans	1½ teaspoons dry mustard
8 cups cold water	1 teaspoon salt
½ cups dark corn syrup	1 teaspoon ground ginger
¼ cup butter or margarine, melted	¼ teaspoon dried thyme
	⅛ teaspoon black pepper
	1 tablespoon minced parsley

1. Wash and pick over beans. Combine beans with the water in a large saucepan, bring to a boil, boil 2 minutes, remove from the heat, cover, and let stand 2 hours.

2. Heat the oven to 350°F.

3. Drain the beans, reserving the liquid, and place them in a 2½-quart casserole or bean pot. In a small bowl combine the remaining ingredients except the parsley and the reserved bean liquid and mix with the beans. Pour liquid over the beans. Cover and bake 1½ hours, or until the beans are tender. For the last 15 minutes remove the cover and let the top brown before serving. Garnish with parsley.

SERVES 6 to 8

Limas with Chilis

Monterey Jack cheese is a creamy cheddarlike cheese popular on the West Coast. You can use a mild Cheddar cheese as a substitute if Monterey Jack is unavailable.

4 cups cooked or canned large
   lima beans
4 ounces Monterey Jack cheese
1 4-ounce can green chilis (4 or
   5 chilis)
2 tablespoons butter or margarine
2 tablespoons minced yellow
   onion

1 teaspoon salt
½ teaspoon dried oregano
½ teaspoon dried basil
⅛ teaspoon black pepper
½ cup sour cream
   Paprika

1. Heat the oven to 350°F.

2. Drain the lima beans, reserving the liquid. Cut the cheese into four or five thin strips and place one inside each chili pepper. Spread the butter or margarine in a 10-inch by 6-inch baking dish and spread ½ of the beans over the bottom. Sprinkle ½ of the onions and seasonings over the beans and arrange the chilis on top. Spread the remaining beans over the chilis; add the remaining onion and seasonings.

3. Stir 1 cup of the bean liquid into the sour cream, and pour over the beans. Bake about 30 minutes, or until the dish is bubbling. Garnish with paprika.

SERVES 4 or 5

Limas in Tomato and Cheese Sauce

Limas in this smooth rich sauce are delicious with broiled meat and with chicken.

3 to 4 cups cooked or canned large
   lima beans, drained
2 tablespoons butter or margarine
1 large yellow onion, peeled and
   minced
1 large clove garlic, peeled and
   minced

1 8-ounce can tomato sauce
1½ teaspoons salt
⅛ teaspoon black pepper
1 3-ounce package cream
   cheese

1. Heat the beans in a saucepan.

2. Melt the butter or margarine in a medium skillet over medium

heat and sauté the onion and garlic until the onion is translucent. Add the tomato sauce, salt, and pepper and simmer 10 minutes, stirring occasionally. Cut the cream cheese into bits and drop into the sauce. Cook, stirring, about 5 minutes until it is melted.

3. Turn the hot beans into a serving dish and pour the sauce over them.

SERVES 4 or 5

Honey-baked Lima Pot

For health-food buffs this is a great variation on the baked bean theme.

2 *cups dry large lima beans*	1 *teaspoon ground ginger*
Water to cover beans	½ *teaspoon dry mustard*
¼ *pound bacon, cut into ½-inch*	¼ *teaspoon ground cloves*
strips	¾ *cup honey*
1 *medium yellow onion, peeled*	
and diced	

1. Wash and pick over the beans. Combine the beans with water to cover in a saucepan, bring to a boil, boil 2 minutes, remove from the heat, cover, and let stand 1 hour.

2. Bring back to a boil and simmer until beans are tender, 45 minutes to 1¼ hours. Drain; reserve the liquid.

3. Heat the oven to 325°F.

4. In a bean pot place half the bacon. Mix the onion with the beans and turn into the bean pot. Mix 1½ cups of the bean cooking liquid with the remaining ingredients and pour over beans. Top with remaining bacon. Bake, covered, 1½ hours. During the last 30 minutes remove the cover so the bacon on top will brown a little. If the mixture dries during the baking, add a little more bean cooking liquid.

SERVES 4 or 5

Baked Limas with Apples

You will hardly taste the apples, but the limas have a different flavor and texture prepared this way.

5 cups cooked or canned large
   lima beans
¼ cup butter or margarine
1 cup chopped yellow onion
4 cups diced, cored, and peeled
   tart apples
½ cup firmly packed light
   brown sugar

1 teaspoon salt
½ teaspoon ground cinnamon
¼ teaspoon ground mace
⅛ cup prepared mustard
⅛ teaspoon black pepper

1. Heat the oven to 350°F.
2. Drain the beans and reserve 1 cup of the liquid. Place the beans in a 2-quart baking dish.
3. Melt 2 tablespoons butter or margarine in a small saucepan over medium heat and sauté the onion about 5 minutes, until translucent. Add the onion to the beans and mix in the remaining ingredients. Dot with the remaining butter and bake, covered, for 2 hours, or until the beans are very tender.

SERVES 6 to 8

Limas and Vegetable Chowder

A thick hearty soup that can be used as a main-course dinner dish when served with hot biscuits, butter, cheese, salad, and fruit. The purpose of the "old" potato is to act as a thickener. In winter, the right season to serve this soup, most potatoes are "old."

1 cup dry small lima beans	*1 carrot, scraped and diced*
4 cups cold water	*2 large stalks celery, with leaves,*
3 tablespoons bacon fat	*chopped*
1 medium yellow onion, peeled	*1 tablespoon minced green pepper*
and chopped	*1 old potato, peeled and grated,*
1 teaspoon salt	*with juice*
⅛ teaspoon black pepper	*4 sprigs parsley, minced*
1 small white turnip, peeled and	*2 cups whole milk*
diced	

1. Wash and pick over the limas. Combine the beans with the water in a large kettle, bring to a boil, boil 2 minutes, remove from the heat, cover, and let stand 1 hour. Return to a boil and cook another 30 minutes.

2. Melt the bacon fat in a large skillet over medium heat, and in it sauté the onion about 5 minutes, until translucent. Add the remaining ingredients, except the milk, and sauté 3 or 4 minutes more. Add to the beans and continue to cook until all the vegetables are tender and the soup is thick. Taste and add more salt and pepper if needed. Add the milk and heat well before serving.

SERVES 6 to 8

Lima Soup with Ham Bone

An easy soup. You can make it in a slow cooker, too; omit soaking the beans and put them in the cooker with the water; then proceed with step 2. Cook on the low-heat setting about 10 to 12 hours. Use rendered fat from the ham roast or use butter or margarine.

1 cup dry large lima beans	*2 tablespoons minced parsley*
6 cups cold water	*½ teaspoon dried thyme*
2 tablespoons rendered ham fat	*1 small bay leaf*
1 medium yellow onion, peeled	*⅛ teaspoon ground cloves*
and minced	*½ teaspoon prepared mustard*
2 large stalks celery, with leaves,	*1 teaspoon salt*
chopped	*¼ teaspoon black pepper*
1 meaty ham bone	

1. Wash and pick over the beans. Combine the beans with water in a large kettle, bring to a boil, boil 2 minutes, remove from the heat, cover, and let stand 1 hour.

2. In a medium skillet melt the ham fat and in it sauté the onion about 5 minutes, until translucent. Add the celery, and sauté 3 or 4 minutes more.

3. Bring the beans back to a boil and add to the beans the ham bone, parsley, thyme, bay leaf, ground cloves, and the contents of the skillet. Cover and simmer 1½ hours, or until the beans are very tender. Check occasionally and add more water if needed. Add mustard, salt, and pepper and simmer another 10 minutes. Garnish with parsley and serve.

SERVES 6 to 8

Lima, Beef, and Barley Soup

A thick old-fashioned soup that can double as the main course.

1 cup dry large lima beans
2 quarts cold water
1 large soup bone
1 pound beef for soup or stew, cubed
½ cup uncooked barley
2 tablespoons butter or margarine
1 cup chopped yellow onion
1 medium bay leaf
1 cup chopped celery with leaves
2 medium carrots, scraped and diced
2 tablespoons minced parsley
2 teaspoons salt
1 teaspoon soy sauce
¼ teaspoon black pepper

1. Wash and pick over the limas. Combine the beans with 1 quart cold water in a large saucepan, bring to a boil, boil 2 minutes, remove from the heat, cover, and let stand 1 hour.

2. Place the soup bone and meat with remaining 1 quart water in a large kettle, bring to a boil, and boil for a few minutes; skim off foam. When the water is clear, add the beans, bean water, and barley.

3. Melt the butter or margarine in a small saucepan over medium heat and sauté the onion about 5 minutes, until translucent. Add

the onion to the soup, rinse out the skillet with a bit of soup, and return to the soup, along with the remaining ingredients. Cook for 2 or 3 hours, or until very thick. If soup reduces too much, add a little more water. Before serving, add salt and pepper if needed and a bit more soy sauce if you wish.

SERVES 6 to 8

Lima Beans, Ham, and Wine Casserole

A hearty main course that relies on leftover baked ham and a bit of the fat rendered from the ham for its special flavor. You can use butter or fat rendered from salt pork instead of ham fat.

1 cup cooked lean ham, minced	1½ cups whole milk
1 large tart apple, cored, peeled and sliced	½ cup dry white wine
	1½ cups grated medium-sharp Cheddar cheese
6 tablespoons fat from a baked ham	1 canned pimiento, chopped
2 tablespoons all-purpose flour	6 cups cooked or canned large lima beans, drained
1½ teaspoons salt	Butter or margarine
⅛ teaspoon black pepper	1 cup bread crumbs
2 teaspoons dry mustard	2 tablespoons chopped parsley
¼ teaspoon dill weed	

1. In a large skillet over medium heat sauté the ham and apple in 2 tablespoons of ham fat until the apple is almost soft. Set aside.

2. In a large saucepan over medium low heat into 3 tablespoons ham fat, stir the flour, salt, pepper, mustard, and dill. When the mixture is smooth, add the milk all at once, and cook, stirring constantly, until the sauce smooths out and thickens. Stir in the wine and cheese, then remove from the heat and mix in the pimiento, beans and ham-apple mixture.

3. Heat the oven to 350°F.

4. Grease a 2½-quart casserole with 1 teaspoon ham fat and turn the bean mixture into it. Bake, uncovered, for 30 minutes. Meanwhile, in the skillet melt 2 teaspoons of the remaining ham fat and sauté the bread crumbs. One minute before the crumbs are

done add the parsley; cook, stirring, 1 minute more, then sprinkle over the casserole and continue to make another 10 or 15 minutes.

SERVES 8

Lima Beans and Pork Chop Casserole

This is nicest when the pork chops are small and thick. Beans should be tender but still firm, not mushy.

3 cups cooked baby lima beans with cooking liquid	*½ cup firmly packed dark brown sugar*
1 28-ounce can tomato purée	*4 tablespoons honey*
4 strips bacon, cut into 1-inch pieces	*2 tablespoons prepared mustard*
	8 pork chops
⅔ cup catsup	*Salt and black pepper to taste*

1. Heat the oven to 325°F.
2. Place the beans and cooking liquid in a large baking dish. Combine the remaining ingredients except the chops, salt, and pepper and pour over the beans.
3. Cut a little fat from the chops, and grease a large skillet with it, warming over medium heat. Lightly brown the chops on each side, then place on top of the beans and press down into the sauce. Cover loosely; bake 1 hour and 15 minutes. Then raise the heat to 425°F., uncover the dish, and bake until the chops are brown on top and the sauce has thickened. Add the salt and pepper.

SERVES 8

Lima Beans and Sausage

A pinch-penny recipe. The sausage gives the beans a meaty flavor and makes this a dish that can be served as a main course. Ground lamb can be used instead of sausage meats. With lamb add ½ teaspoon dry thyme instead of sage and include any roast drippings you have (after spooning off the fat) to strengthen the flavor.

1⅓ cups dry large lima beans
    Water to cover beans
½ pound sausage meat
1 small yellow onion, peeled
    and chopped
1 large clove garlic, peeled and
    minced

⅓ cup all-purpose flour
1½ teaspoons salt
¼ teaspoon dried sage
⅛ teaspoon black pepper
1 cup evaporated milk

1. ·Wash and pick over the beans. Combine the beans with water in a large saucepan. Bring to a boil, boil 2 minutes, remove from the heat, cover, and let stand for 1 hour. Return the beans to the heat, cover, and boil for 1 hour. Add more water as needed.

2. Set a large skillet over medium-high heat, and while the skillet is still cool, press the sausage meat into it. When the sausage is partially browned, scrape it to one side and add the onion and garlic. Cook until the onion is translucent and the sausage lightly browned. Drain off all but ⅓ cup fat. Lower the heat and push the sausage and onion to one side. Stir the flour, salt, sage, and pepper into the fat, then stir in the evaporated milk; work quickly to make a smooth paste. Use a colander to drain the bean cooking liquid into the skillet, and cool, stirring as the sauce thickens. Add cooked beans and mix well.

SERVES 3 to 4

Lima Meat Loaf with Tomato Sauce

I make this with leftover limas, leftover ham, and leftover meat sauce or tomato sauce from a spaghetti dinner.

6 tablespoons butter or
    margarine
1 cup cooked or canned large
    lima beans, drained
¼ cup chili sauce
1 cup minced leftover ham
2 eggs, slightly beaten
½ teaspoon prepared mustard

1 large Spanish onion, peeled
    and minced
1 cup cracker or dry bread
    crumbs
1 teaspoon salt
⅛ teaspoon black pepper
1 8-ounce can tomato sauce

1. Heat the oven to 350°F.

2. Melt the butter or margarine in a very small saucepan. In a large bowl, using a potato masher, mash the beans thoroughly. Add 3 tablespoons of the melted butter, and the chili sauce, and mash and whip the beans into a purée.

3. With a fork, beat the ham into the eggs. Add the mustard and beat into the puréed beans. Mix in the onion and the cracker or bread crumbs. Add the salt and pepper, using additional amounts to taste. Shape into a loaf and set on a greased baking pan. Drizzle the remaining melted butter over the top of the loaf. Bake 30 minutes.

4. Heat the tomato sauce and serve over individual slices of loaf.

SERVES 4

Lima Beans and Leg of Lamb

In the part of France I come from, the Vendée, this is most often made with small white beans; but since I haven't always had the time to cook small white beans, I've gotten into the habit of using dry or frozen limas instead.

2 cups dry baby lima beans	2 medium yellow onions, peeled
6 cups cold water	and minced
3 medium cloves garlic, peeled	2 large sprigs parsley
1 4- or 5-pound leg of lamb	1 bay leaf
2 tablespoons softened butter	¼ teaspoon dried thyme
1 teaspoon curry powder	3 shallots, peeled and minced
½ teaspoon salt	1 medium tomato, peeled and
¼ teaspoon black pepper	chopped
1 cup beef bouillon or stock	

1. Wash and pick over the beans. Combine the beans with the water in a large saucepan, bring to a boil, boil 2 minutes, remove from the heat, cover, and let stand 1 hour.

2. Heat the oven to 425°F.

3. Cut 2 cloves garlic into long slivers. With a sharp knife point, prick small holes in the outer portion of the lamb and insert the

garlic slivers. In a cup mix butter, curry powder, salt, and pepper to a smooth paste and spread over the lamb; place in the preheated oven. Bake, uncovered, for about 20 minutes. Pour ½ cup beef bouillon or stock into the pan, lower the heat to 350°F. and bake about 1½ hours more, basting occasionally. About 20 minutes before it is done, add the remaining bouillon. If you prefer the lamb well done, cook about 20 minutes more.

4. Meanwhile, return beans to the stove top burner and add the onion and 1 sliced clove garlic, parsley, bay leaf, and thyme. Bring to a boil, cover, and simmer for about 1½ hours, or until the beans are tender but not breaking up.

5. When the beans are done, drain, reserving the liquid.

6. When the roast is done, remove it from the roasting pan. Spoon about 2 tablespoons drippings from the roasting pan into a small saucepan over medium heat, add the minced shallot and the tomato, and sauté until the shallot is translucent.

7. Add the sautéed shallot and tomato to the roasting pan juices, with ¼ cup of bean cooking liquid (if the bouillon has all evaporated), and scrape and stir to make gravy. If it is thin, boil over stove top burner, stirring, for a few minutes. Taste the sauce and add more salt and pepper if desired. Pour about half the sauce into a gravy boat and keep warm. Turn the beans into the roasting pan and combine well with the pan juices. Turn onto a serving platter, set the roast on top, and serve.

SERVES 8

Lima Bean Fruitcake

This is a south-of-the-border fiesta cake that can also be made with pinto beans. It's rather like applesauce cake.

CAKE:

2 cups freshly cooked baby
   lima beans
   Bean cooking liquid
1 cup sifted cake flour
1 teaspoon baking soda
1 teaspoon ground cinnamon
½ teaspoon ground cloves
½ teaspoon ground allspice
½ teaspoon ground mace
½ teaspoon salt
½ cup butter or margarine at
   room temperature
1 cup firmly packed light brown
   sugar
2 teaspoons vanilla

1 egg
2 cups chopped, cored, and
   peeled tart apples
3 tablespoons cake flour
1 cup dark raisins
½ cup chopped walnuts

SAUCE:

3 tablespoons butter
3 tablespoons all-purpose flour
1 cup boiling water
1 cup firmly packed light brown
   sugar
⅛ teaspoon salt
1 teaspoon vanilla

1. Heat oven to 350°F.

2. In a large flat-bottom bowl mash the beans with about 2 cups bean liquid, enough so you can beat the beans smooth without having them runny. Keep warm.

3. Sift together the flour, soda, cinnamon, cloves, allspice, mace, and salt.

4. Cream the butter and beat in the brown sugar. Beat in the vanilla and the egg. Beat in the whipped beans; then add the dry ingredients a little at a time. Fold in the apples, raisins, and nuts. Turn into a greased and floured 9-inch tube pan. Bake for 50 to 60 minutes, or until a straw inserted in the center comes out clean. Cool in the pan on a rack for 10 minutes, then turn out of the pan and finish cooling on the rack.

5. Melt the butter for the sauce in a saucepan over medium heat and stir in the flour to make a smooth paste. Add the boiling water all at once. Stir in the brown sugar, salt, and vanilla, and continue to cook, stirring, until thick. Let cool slightly.

6. Set the cake on a serving plate and slowly pour the topping over it.

SERVES 10 to 12

9

Pink Beans and Pintos

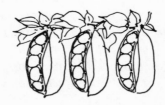

The pinks and the pintos are my favorite beans, especially for serving plain with butter.

Most of the recipes here can be made with either pinks or pintos, but a few I think are slightly better if they are done with pinks, and I have recommended pinks for these.

The Pinto or Pink Bean Dip (pages 91–92) is typical of a number of recipes for making highly seasoned bean mashes and dips and can be made with almost any of the other colored beans. With plain white beans, or blackeyes or yellow eyes, however, it might be a bit bland.

In this and in the other bean chapters you'll find several variations on beans with chili and chili con carne sauce. Chili enjoys almost as much popularity in America as does the hamburger, especially in the South and West. Experiment, and when you find the one you prefer, use that recipe with either pink, pinto, light, or dark red kidney beans, red beans, or almost any other beans you have handy—except the whites. The pinks are the beans we most often use for American versions of Mexican cooking.

In this chapter you'll find some recipes that really are fun to experiment with. There's a Pink Bean and Rice Pie (pages 96–97) made with rice crust, and there's Pink Bean Whip (pages 94–95), a way of making mashed beans that can be used with any of the mealy beans, including the whites. Roasted Pink Beans (page 91) is a basic recipe for roasting *cooked* beans to eat like peanuts. (In chapter 6 you'll find a recipe for Roasted Soybeans—page 53— that have *not* been cooked.)

Sweet Pink Bean Tarts (page 106), the last recipe in this chapter, are really good. The basic recipe is one familiar to afficionados of pumpkin pie. You can make this with any flavorful mealy bean.

To my mind, fresh cooked and mashed pink beans come close to being as good as mashed roasted chestnuts.

Roasted Pink Beans

Roasted salted beans were something my French grandmother made for her children. They may not be as irresistible as peanuts, but they're fun. Try this some time when you have a handful of firm-cooked beans left over; and if you like it, use as a substitute for peanuts. Or, chop the roasted beans and sprinkle over casseroles.

1 teaspoon vegetable oil   *Salt to taste*
2 cups cooked pink beans, firm

   1. Heat the oven to 200°F.
   2. Oil a flat roasting pan and sprinkle the beans over the surface. Place in the oven and bake 1 hour, or until lightly browned. Sprinkle with salt and serve warm or cold. (An alternate method is to roll the beans around in a lightly oiled skillet over a medium heat until they are lightly browned.)

SERVES 3

Pinto or Pink Bean Dip

This is a Mexican way with beans—not refried, but "well fried." Great for stuffing tacos and as a dip for corn chips. Mexican cooks use oil instead of butter.

2 cups cooked or canned, pinto   ½ teaspoon dried cumin
    or pink beans, drained   Salt to taste
1 small clove garlic, peeled   1 tablespoon vegetable oil
    and crushed   Grated Monterey Jack or
½ teaspoon chili powder   Cheddar cheese

1. Place the beans in a large flat-bottom bowl with the garlic, chili, and cumin. With a potato masher mash the beans thoroughly. Taste and add a little salt if needed.

2. Heat the oil in a large skillet over high heat; it should be very hot. Spoon the beans into the skillet and keep turning and mashing them as they cook. In 5 to 10 minutes, when the mixture is well fried, turn back into the bowl and stir in grated cheese to taste.

SERVES 4

Pink Beans and Red Cabbage Salad

These combined garden vegetables are nice served on a bed of frilly endive or escarole leaves.

3 cups cooked or canned pink   1 cup vegetable oil
    or pinto beans, drained   ¼ cup cider vinegar
1 cup grated celery   ⅛ teaspoon dry mustard
1 cup grated radishes   ½ teaspoon granulated sugar
1 cup grated cucumber   1½ teaspoon salt
2 cups shredded red cabbage   ⅛ teaspoon black pepper
¼ cup grated yellow onion   ½ cup mayonnaise

1. In a very large bowl combine the beans, celery, radishes, cucumber, and cabbage.

2. For dressing, mix remaining ingredients in the blender until smooth. Pour the dressing over the vegetables and toss until thoroughly mixed. Cover and chill for several hours before serving. Check seasonings and add more salt if needed.

SERVES 8 to 10

Pink Bean Salad with Chicory

If you like garlic, this one is for you. Fresh-cooked beans are tossed in the dressing while still warm from cooking. If the beans are canned, warm them in their liquid, then drain.

2 cups chicory leaves cut into bite-size pieces
2 cups cooked or canned pink or pinto beans, drained
½ cup vegetable oil
2 tablespoons cider vinegar
½ teaspoon salt
⅛ teaspoon black pepper
¼ teaspoon prepared mustard
Pinch of granulated sugar
2 large cloves garlic, peeled and minced very fine
4 tablespoons minced fresh parsley
Whole chicory leaves

Place the bite-size chicory pieces into a large bowl and add the drained beans. For dressing mix remaining ingredients except garlic, parsley, and whole chicory leaves in the blender. Stir in the garlic and toss the dressing with the beans and chicory. When well tossed, add the parsley and toss again. Serve in a salad bowl lined with frilly green outer chicory leaves.

SERVES 4 to 6

Minestrone with Beans

This is made with beef shanks and is hearty enough to be a meal all by itself. Serve with hot rolls and a salad. The cabbage does not have to be shredded in a shredder—it can be thinly sliced with a sharp knife.

1 cup dry pink or pinto beans
5 cups cold water
2 pounds beef shank, cross cut
2 tablespoons vegetable oil or
   beef roast drippings
1 16-ounce can whole tomatoes
3 tablespoons tomato paste
½ medium head cabbage,
   shredded
1 large carrot, scraped and sliced
1 large yellow onion, peeled
   and sliced
2 medium cloves garlic, peeled
   and sliced

½ tablespoon salt
1 small bay leaf
2 teaspoons dried basil
¼ teaspoon ground thyme
¼ teaspoon black pepper
2 beef bouillon cubes
⅓ cup elbow macaroni
1 10-ounce package frozen cut
   Italian-style (or plain)
   green beans
Grated Parmesan cheese

1. Wash and pick over the beans. Combine the beans with the water in a big soup kettle, bring to a boil, boil 2 minutes, remove from the heat, and let stand 1 hour.

2. Brown the beef shanks in oil in a large Dutch oven or kettle, over medium high heat, turning often. Add the beans and bean liquid, scrape up the pan juices, cover, and simmer 30 minutes.

3. Drain the tomato liquid into the kettle, reserving the tomatoes, and add to the kettle the tomato paste, cabbage, carrot, onion, garlic, salt, seasonings, and bouillon cubes. Cover and simmer 1½ to 2 hours, or until the meat is falling off the bones. Check occasionally and add more liquid if needed. Remove the shanks, cut the meat into small pieces, and return to the soup. Cut up and add the reserved tomatoes. Add the macaroni and green beans. Simmer until the macaroni and beans are tender. Serve with Parmesan cheese.

SERVES 8

Pink Bean Whip

This is nicest if the beans have just finished cooking—better than if they've been canned or frozen or reheated.

4 cups cooked pink beans, drained   ½ teaspoon salt
   Bean cooking liquid   ⅛ teaspoon black pepper
4 to 6 tablespoons softened butter

Place the just-cooked beans in a large bowl and whip with the electric beater on low. As the beater fluffs the beans, add a little hot cooking liquid to make beating easier. When the beans are all broken, add the butter and continue beating till the beans have absorbed all the butter. If they seem dry, add a little more hot bean liquid and beat again. Season with salt and pepper and serve very hot.

SERVES 8

Chili Beans and Cheese

2 cups dry pink or pinto beans   ¼. teaspoon black pepper
7 cups cold water   1 small yellow onion, peeled
¼ pound salt pork   and minced
2 teaspoons salt   Grated Cheddar cheese
3 teaspoons chili powder

1. Wash the beans and pick them over. Combine the beans with the water, in a saucepan, bring to a boil, boil 2 minutes, remove from the heat, cover, and let stand 1 hour.

2. Score the salt pork and poke it down into the beans. Cover and bring back to boil; reduce the heat, and simmer 2 hours, stirring occasionally. Add more water if needed. Add the salt, chili, pepper, and onion and cook 30 minutes more, or until the beans are very tender. Before serving, garnish the dish with a light sprinkling of grated Cheddar cheese.

SERVES 6

Pink Beans and Cabbage, Spanish Style

This is an adaptation of a Spanish recipe. The method for cooking the beans is different and fun to try. It makes use of leftover rendered fat and the bone from a baked ham.

2⅔ cups (1 pound) dry pink or
    pinto beans
   Water to cover beans
3 tablespoons fat from a ham
    roast
   Ham bone with meat
3 cups cold water
½ small white cabbage, cored
    and sliced thick

1 teaspoon salt
¼ teaspoon black pepper
2 tablespoons olive oil
1 medium yellow onion, peeled
    and chopped
1 large clove garlic, peeled and
    chopped
1 sprig parsley, minced

1. Wash and pick over the beans and place in a large Dutch oven or kettle. Add cold water until it reaches an inch above the beans. Add the ham fat and the ham bone. Turn the heat high and bring the water to a boil. Add 1 cup of cold water. Repeat two more times, using 3 cups cold water in all. Cover, lower heat, and simmer 1½ hours.

2. Mix in the cabbage, salt, and pepper and continue to cook until the beans are tender but not yet breaking up, about 20 to 30 minutes.

3. Heat the oil in a medium skillet on medium heat and sauté the onion, garlic, and parsley until the onion is golden. Mix into the beans. Remove the ham bone and mince the meat from it and return to the beans.

SERVES 4 to 6

Pink Beans and Rice Pie

Save cooked rice to make the pie crust, and fill it with this tasty pink bean mixture. This isn't a dessert pie—it's a luncheon, complete when served with tossed green salad.

1⅓ cups cooked white rice
2 tablespoons melted butter or
    margarine
2 tablespoons vegetable oil
1 small yellow onion, peeled
    and minced
1 medium carrot, scraped and
    grated

1 medium stalk celery, minced
2 to 3 cups cooked or canned
    pink or pinto beans, drained
1 teaspoon ground cumin
3 tablespoons soy sauce
   Salt and pepper to taste
⅓ cup grated sharp Cheddar

1. Heat the oven to 350°F.

2. Place the rice in a bowl and mix the melted butter or margarine with it. With your hands pat it into an 8-inch pie plate to make a shell.

3. Heat the oil in a medium skillet over medium heat and sauté the onion, carrot, and celery until the onion is translucent. Combine with beans, cumin, and soy sauce. Taste and add salt and pepper if desired. Scoop into the pie crust and bake about 25 minutes. Sprinkle the cheese over the top and bake 5 to 10 minutes more, or until cheese is bubbly.

SERVES 5 to 6

Pink Beans with Salt Pork

This is a very simple but flavorful way to prepare pink beans; and it's easy to do in the slow cooker. Just place all the ingredients into the pot except the salt and cook until done—10 to 12 hours on the low-heat setting. Add the salt later.

2⅔ cups (1 pound) dry pink or   1 pound salt pork, cut into 1-inch
    pinto beans   pieces
2 quarts cold water   Salt to taste
1 large yellow onion, peeled
    and chopped

Wash and pick over the beans, drain them, and combine them with the water in a large kettle that has a lid. Stir in the onion and the salt pork. Cover and bring to a boil. Lower the heat and simmer until the beans are tender and most of the water is absorbed, about 2 hours. If there's a lot of cooking liquid left when the beans are tender, uncover for the last few minutes of cooking. Taste and add salt if needed.

SERVES 8

Quick Bean Casserole for a Crowd

This is a quick and easy recipe that takes only 20 minutes to put together.

12 cups cooked or canned pink or pinto beans, drained (reserve liquid)
12 slices bacon, halved
2 large yellow onions, peeled and diced

¼ cup firmly packed light brown sugar
½ teaspoon black pepper
3 dashes Tabasco sauce
1 bottle catsup
1 cup ale

1. Heat the oven to 350°F.
2. Place the beans in a 3- or 4-quart casserole or bean pot.
3. Place the bacon strips in a large skillet, turn on the heat to medium, and cook just enough to render a few tablespoons of fat. Remove and drain the bacon. Reserve the fat.
4. Sauté the onions in the fat in the same skillet over medium heat until translucent and stir in the remaining ingredients. Scrape over the beans. Mix gently and top with partially cooked bacon strips. Cover and bake 1 hour. Check occasionally and add water if pot is drying. About 15 minutes before baking is over, remove the cover, and let top brown slightly.

SERVES 12 to 16

Pink Beans and Sausages

½ pound link sausages
2 cups water
2 tablespoons butter or margarine
1 cup chopped yellow onion
1 large clove garlic, peeled and minced
4 cups cooked or canned pink or pinto beans, drained

⅓ cup firmly packed light brown sugar
½ cup catsup
2 tablespoons cider vinegar
2 tablespoons prepared mustard
2 teaspoons chili powder
3 cups hot cooked white rice

1. Simmer the sausages in the water in a medium saucepan for about 5 minutes. Remove the sausages, drain them, and cut into thin slices.

2. Turn sausages into a large skillet with the butter or margarine, onion, and garlic, and over medium heat, sauté until the onions are translucent. Add the remaining ingredients except rice, and cook, stirring occasionally, until the beans are heated through, about 15 minutes. Serve over hot rice.

SERVES 6

Pink Beans, Rice, and Ham Hock

In Creole Louisiana, red beans and rice were traditional fare on Mondays. The bone from the Sunday ham went into the dish, and it cooked forever on the back of the stove. You can make this in a slow cooker, starting with step 2, cooking 10 to 12 hours on the low-heat setting.

2 cups dry pink or pinto beans	*2 medium cloves garlic, peeled*
5 cups water	*and minced*
1 ham hock (about 1 pound), split	*⅛ teaspoon black pepper*
1 large yellow onion, peeled and	*1 teaspoon salt*
minced	*4 cups cooked white rice*
1 large stalk celery, with leaves,	*½ cup minced green onions*
minced	

1. Wash and pick over the beans, and soak them overnight in water.

2. Bring the beans to a boil, add the ham hock, onion, celery, garlic, and pepper. Bring to a boil and simmer until the beans are tender, 1½ to 2½ hours. Add water as needed if the beans dry out. Mash a few beans into the cooking liquid to thicken it. Remove the ham hock, dice the meat, discard the bone, return the meat to the beans, and mix well together. Add salt, taste, and add more if needed.

3. Into soup plates spoon a mound of rice, ladle beans and ham over it, and serve with green onion on the side.

SERVES 6 to 8

Pink Beans and Spare Ribs

You could use red beans for this, too.

1 tablespoon bacon drippings	½ teaspoon dried thyme
1½ pounds spareribs, cut into 1-inch pieces	1 8-ounce can tomato sauce
	2 teaspoons salt
1 large Spanish onion, peeled and sliced	⅛ teaspoon black pepper
	1 tablespoon cider vinegar
3 cups cooked or canned pink or pinto beans	

1. Heat the oven to 350°F.
2. Melt the bacon drippings in a large skillet over medium heat and sauté the spareribs until well browned all over—10 to 15 minutes. Remove the spareribs and keep warm. Sauté the onion in the remaining fat until translucent; add beans and bean liquid and remaining ingredients.
3. Arrange the spareribs in a 2½-quart casserole and pour over them the bean mixture. Bake, partially covered, about 45 minutes, until the spareribs are tender. If sauce is thin, uncover for last 15 minutes of baking.

SERVES 4 to 5

Pink Beans and Chili Con Carne

Ripe olives and unsweetened chocolate give this mild chili a flavor you usually only find in Latin America. Pitted ripe olives in cans are sold in most supermarkets. One-half ounce of chocolate is half of a 1-ounce wrapped square. It's easiest to grate if it is chilled first.

4 tablespoons vegetable oil	1½ teaspoon salt
1 pound beef stew meat, cut into ½-inch pieces, boneless	½ teaspoon ground thyme
	½ teaspoon ground cumin
½ pound pork shoulder, cut into ½-inch pieces	1½ cups cold water
	1 cup pitted ripe olives
1½ cups chopped yellow onion	1 8-ounce can tomato sauce
1 cup seeded, diced green pepper	½ ounce unsweetened chocolate, grated
2 large cloves garlic, peeled and minced	2 cups cooked or canned pink or pinto beans
1 tablespoon chili powder	3 cups hot cooked white rice

1. Heat the oil in a large Dutch oven over medium high heat and sauté the meats until well browned all over—10 to 15 minutes. Add the onion, green pepper, and garlic and cook about 10 minutes until the onion is translucent. Stir in the seasonings and add the water, scraping up the pan juices. Bring to a boil, then reduce the heat, cover, and simmer 45 minutes. Add the olives, tomato sauce, and chocolate and simmer, uncovered, until thickened, about 25 minutes.

2. Heat the beans, then drain the liquid. Alternate mounds (about ½ cup of each) of beans and rice on the outside of a big flat-bottom vegetable dish and spoon the chili into the center.

SERVES 6 to 8

Texas Chili Casserole

This resembles Mexican chili, but corn chips and cheese give it a distinctly American flavor.

1 tablespoon vegetable oil
1½ pounds ground beef
1 tablespoon salt
⅛ teaspoon black pepper
1 large clove garlic, peeled and minced
½ teaspoon ground cumin
1 28-ounce can whole tomatoes

½ teaspoon granulated sugar
¼ cup water
2 cups cooked or canned pink or pinto beans
3 tablespoons chili powder
3 cups corn chips
½ cup minced yellow onion
1 cup grated American cheese

1. Heat the oil in a large saucepan and brown the meat well. Add the salt, pepper, garlic, cumin, tomatoes, and sugar and scrape up the pan juices. Stir, cooking at slow boil (a little faster than simmer, a little less than a full rolling boil) until the sauce has thickened, about 25 minutes.

2. Heat the oven to 350°F.

3. Add the beans and chili powder to the sauce and continue to stir and cook another few minutes. Place 2 cups of corn chips in a 2-quart casserole. Mix the onion and water, sprinkle the onion on top and ½ the grated cheese. Pour the hot

chili sauce into the casserole, and top with the remaining corn chips and cheese. Bake for 15 to 20 minutes.

SERVES 6 to 8

Easy Chili and Pink Beans

Here's a way to make a really fast mild chili. If you like hot chilis, double the quantity of chili powder.

2 *tablespoons vegetable oil*
1 *pound ground beef*
1 *16-ounce can tomato sauce for
    spaghetti*
2 *teaspoons chili powder or to
    taste*

1 *large clove garlic, peeled
    and minced*
½ *teaspoon salt*
1 *teaspoon ground cumin*
2 *cups cooked or canned pink
    or pinto beans*

Heat the oil in a large skillet over medium-high heat and sauté the meat, stirring, until the meat is crumbled and brown all over. Stir in all ingredients except the beans and simmer, covered, 20 minutes. Add the beans and simmer 10 more minutes.

SERVES 4 to 6

Seasoned Beans and Meatballs

A savory stew, very thick and full of good things. Great with crisp rolls and butter, and a tossed green salad. This begins with dry beans.

1½ cups dry pink or pinto beans
4 cups cold water
2 tablespoons vegetable oil
1 cup minced yellow onion
2 large cloves garlic, peeled and minced
1 pound ground beef
1 teaspoon each of summer savory, basil, sweet marjoram, and parsley, combined
1 teaspoon salt
¼ teaspoon black pepper
¼ cup whipping cream, light cream, or evaporated milk
½ cup dry bread crumbs
1 16-ounce can tomato sauce
2 medium potatoes, peeled and diced
2 medium carrots, scraped and cut into ¼-inch rounds
1 1¼-ounce package taco seasoning mix
1 8¾-ounce can whole kernel corn
Grated sharp Cheddar cheese

1. Wash and pick over the beans. Combine with the water in a medium saucepan, bring to a boil, boil 2 minutes, remove from the heat, cover, and let stand 1 hour. Return to the heat and cook until tender, 1½ to 2 hours.

2. Heat the oil in a large skillet over medium heat, sauté ⅔ cup of the onion, and the garlic, until the onion turns translucent. Place the meat in a large bowl. Scrape the cooked onion into the meat, add the seasonings, salt, pepper, and cream and mix well. Stir in the bread crumbs. Shape meat into balls, 1 inch in diameter. Place them in the hot skillet; sauté, swirling the skillet so the meatballs roll, until meatballs are brown all over.

3. With a slotted spoon remove the meatballs and sauté ⅓ cup minced onion until translucent. Add the onion to the beans with tomato sauce, potatoes, carrots, and taco seasoning. Simmer, covered, about 20 minutes, or until the carrots are half tender. If beans are drying, add a little water. Add the meat balls and undrained corn kernels. Cover, and simmer 10 minutes more, or until potatoes and carrots are completely cooked. Taste and add more salt and pepper if needed. Sprinkle each serving with grated cheese.

SERVES 8

Pink Beans and Vegetable Stew

A nice mélange of root vegetables with pink beans in a cream sauce.

1 teaspoon vegetable oil
5 tablespoons butter
1 cup peeled and minced yellow
    onion
1 cup scraped and grated carrot
1 cup scraped and grated
    parsnip

4 cups cooked or canned pink
    or pinto beans
    Whole milk
3 tablespoons all-purpose flour
1 teaspoon salt
¼ teaspoon ground nutmeg
    Salt and black pepper to taste

1. Heat the oil and 2 tablespoons butter in a large Dutch oven over medium heat and saute the onion, carrot, and parsnip until the onion is translucent. Add the beans and bean liquid, cover, and simmer 45 minutes. Drain the cooking liquid and reserve; if there aren't 2 cups, add whole milk to make 2 cups.

2. Melt 3 tablespoons butter in a medium saucepan over low heat and stir in the flour to make a smooth paste. Add the warm bean liquid all at once, and stir quickly to smooth the sauce. Add the salt and nutmeg. Simmer, stirring, until the sauce thickens. Mix with the vegetables. Taste and add more salt, and the pepper, if desired.

SERVES 6 to 8

Pink Beans and Tortillas

Tortillas are currently being sold by the can in supermarkets all across the country. There are about 18 tortillas to the can.

1 tablespoon vegetable oil
¾ pound ground beef
¾ cup chopped yellow onion
1 8-ounce can whole tomatoes
1 teaspoon salt
1 teaspoon chili powder
¼ teaspoon Tabasco sauce

1 8-ounce can tomato sauce
2 cups cooked or canned pink
    or pinto beans, drained
18 tortillas
1 cup shredded, medium-sharp
    Cheddar cheese

1. Heat the oil in a large skillet over medium high heat and sauté the beef, stirring and turning, until beef is brown. Add the onion and cook until the onion is translucent and the meat quite brown all over. Add the tomatoes, salt, chili, and Tabasco and stir well to scrape up pan juices. Remove from the heat. Stir in the tomato sauce. Mash the beans with a potato masher until they are pureed, and combine with the meat.

2. Heat the oven to 350°F.

3. Butter or oil a 1½-quart casserole or round baking dish, and spread a layer of meat and bean mixture over the bottom. Cover with a layer of tortillas. Continue layering meat-and-bean mixture and tortillas until all are used. End with a layer of tortillas and top with cheese. Bake uncovered for 20 to 25 minutes.

SERVES 6 to 8

Pink Beans, Tostadas, and Cheese for a Crowd

Tostadas are commonly sold in supermarkets in 5-ounce packages, about 12 to a package.

2 tablespoons vegetable oil	Bean cooking liquid
2 large yellow onions, peeled and chopped	12 ounces canned tomato purée
	3 tablespoons chili powder
2 large cloves garlic, peeled and minced	1 teaspoon salt
	1 teaspoon ground cumin
2 pounds ground beef	¼ teaspoon black pepper
2 medium green peppers, seeded and chopped	¼ cup grated Cheddar cheese
	2 cups finely shredded red cabbage
4 cups cooked or canned pink or pinto beans	24 tostadas

1. Heat the oil in a large skillet over medium high heat and sauté the onions and garlic until translucent. Add the beef and stir and cook until the meat is broken up and brown all over. Add the remaining ingredients except cabbage and tostadas, mix well, cover, lower the heat, and simmer about 30 minutes, or until the sauce has thickened. If it dries, add a little hot water.

2. To serve, heat the tostadas following package directions and pour chili over each. Top with a bit of shredded red cabbage.

SERVES 8 to 12

Sweet Pink Bean Tarts for a Crowd

Beans as a dessert are rather rare, except in the Orient, where they do turn up as bean paste in sweets, and in South America, notably Chile. This filling for tarts can be used to make a pie instead. It's a bit like butternut squash pie.

3 cups cooked or canned pink beans, drained
1 13-ounce can evaporated milk
2 eggs
1 cup firmly packed light brown sugar
1 teaspoon ground cinnamon

½ teaspoon grated nutmeg
¼ teaspoon ground cloves
¼ teaspoon salt
Pastry for a two-crust pie
Butter or margarine
Whole milk
½ pint whipped cream, sweetened

1. Heat oven to 450°F.
2. In a large flat-bottom bowl mash the beans with a potato masher and measure out 2 cups. In a blender, blend a little at a time with a portion of the evaporated milk, until smooth. Beat the eggs until thick and lemon colored, and beat in the sugar, cinnamon, nutmeg, cloves, and salt. Beat in the mashed beans.
3. Roll the pastry ⅛ inch thick and cut into rounds with a floured 4-inch cookie cutter. Butter a 12-cup (3-inch diameter) muffin pan. Fit pastry snugly into the cups. Trim the shells to fit. Fill shells ⅔ full with bean mixture. Moisten pastry edges with milk (helps them to brown nicely).
4. Place in the oven and bake *15 minutes only*. Reduce the heat to 300°F. and bake 45 minutes more, or until a knife inserted in the center of one cup comes out clean.
5. Allow the tarts to cool for about 10 minutes, lift from cups, and serve with whipped cream.

SERVES 12

10

Small and Large White Beans

The small white beans are perhaps the best known beans in the East. Boston Baked Beans (page 111), made with small white (navy or pea) beans, are very famous indeed. But did you know there are several variations on this? If cooked with onions and a bit of bay leaf, the dish is considered Connecticut style; baked with maple syrup instead of molasses, it's Vermont style; baked with chili or catsup and extra brown sugar, it's New Hampshire style but similar to the way baked beans are flavored in the West. A few more variations are presented on the following pages.

You can use almost any white bean I can think of—marrow, large white, Great Northern—in the place of the small whites. Other whites usually cook faster than the small whites, which are one of the slowest cooking. So do soak small whites, following package directions, or in water overnight or 10 to 12 hours, or as directed in the recipes (see also pages 40–41). Several of these recipes can be made in a slow cooker, but be sure to soak the beans first or start with beans that have been cooked until at least partially tender.

The white beans have a buttery mealy quality and a very pleasant flavor, but they are blander than the more colorful beans. They are good in meaty stews and are used more often with lamb and pork products than some of the other bean varieties.

White Bean Salad, Greek Style

Here's a simple, easy bean salad, great with Greek or Italian dishes.

1 medium clove garlic, peeled
  and minced
1 teaspoon salt
½ teaspoon black pepper
3 tablespoons olive oil or
  vegetable oil

1 tablespoon red wine vinegar
2½ cups cooked or canned small
  white beans, drained
¼ cup finely minced parsley
1 stalk celery, washed and
  minced very fine

Sprinkle minced garlic clove in the bottom of a wooden salad bowl, sprinkle salt over it, and mash the salt into the garlic until it becomes garlic salt. Add the pepper, oil, and vinegar and beat to combine the ingredients. Add the beans, parsley, and celery and toss. Add more salt and pepper to taste.

SERVES 4 to 5

Bean Soup, Capitol Hill Style

Save leftover mashed potatoes and a bone from a cooked smoked ham to make this tasty soup. The more meat left on the ham bone, the richer the soup. Here we are using the overnight soak, but you could quick-soak instead (see pages 40–41).

2⅔ cups (1 pound) dried small
  white beans
3 quarts cold water
1 ham bone with bits of cooked
  ham on it
3 whole cloves
3 tablespoons butter or
  margarine
3 medium yellow onions, peeled
  and chopped

1 medium carrot, scraped and
  diced
1 medium bunch celery with
  leaves, washed and chopped
1 large clove garlic, peeled and
  minced
½ cup mashed potatoes
¼ cup fresh finely minced parsley
Salt and black pepper to taste

1. Soak the beans in the water overnight or for 10 to 12 hours. Place the soaked beans with the water, ham bone, and cloves in a large soup kettle, cover, and boil over medium heat for 2 hours.

2. Melt the butter or margarine in a heavy saucepan and sauté the onions, carrot, celery, and garlic until the onions are translucent. Scrape into the kettle; rinse out the saucepan with bean broth and add to the kettle. Stir the mashed potatoes into the soup, add 1 tablespoon parsley, cover, and cook 1 hour more.

3. Before serving, remove the ham bone, scrape the meat from it, dice the meat, and return to the kettle. Discard the bone and cloves. Simmer another 10 minutes. Add salt and pepper. Garnish with remaining parsley.

SERVES 6 to 8

Beef Bone Soup

Beef rib roast costs are rather high at this writing, but the pain of the price can be soothed if you use the bone and bits of meat and fat clinging to it to make this very good bean soup. Include any drippings left in the beef roasting pan. If you don't want to make the soup the day after you've eaten the roast, freeze the bone, carefully wrapped in freezer foil or sealed in freezer-wrap paper.

1½ cups dry small white beans	¼ teaspoon dried marjoram
2 quarts cold water	1 medium to small yellow onion,
Beef bones	peeled and chopped
1½ teaspoons salt	1 cup diced celery
1 small clove garlic, peeled and minced	1 medium carrot, scraped and diced
¼ teaspoon black pepper	1 28-ounce can whole tomatoes
1 small bay leaf	and liquid
¼ teaspoon dried thyme	

1. Wash and pick over the beans. Combine the beans with the water in a saucepan, bring them to a boil, boil 2 minutes, remove from the heat, cover, and let stand for 1 hour. Drain the beans, reserving the liquid.

2. In a large kettle bring the bean liquid and the bones to a boil, skim the foam, then add the beans, salt, garlic, pepper, bay leaf, thyme, and marjoram. Cover and simmer for 2 hours, or until beans are tender.

3. Remove the bone, cut the meat from it, chop the meat, and return the meat to the soup along with the onion, celery, carrot, and tomatoes. Cover, bring to a boil, then lower the heat and simmer 40 minutes. Add salt and pepper if needed.

SERVES 6

Lamb and Bean Soup, Near East Style

Step 2 can be done in a slow cooker: Eliminate step 1, use ⅔ as much water, cook on a low-heat setting 10 to 12 hours, and follow step 3 shortly before it is time to serve the dish.

⅔ *cup dry small white beans*
2 *quarts cold water*
2 *pounds lamb stew meat, cut into 1-inch pieces*
2 *large yellow onions, peeled and diced*
¼ *teaspoon black pepper*

½ *teaspoon dried thyme*
1½ *teaspoons salt*
¼ *cup olive oil*
3 *tablespoons all-purpose flour*
2 *tablespoons tomato paste*
2 *tablespoons strained lemon juice*

1. Wash and pick over the beans. Combine the beans with water in a large soup kettle, bring to a boil, boil 2 minutes, remove from the heat, cover, and let stand 1 hour.

2. Add the meat and the onions, pepper, and thyme, cover, bring to a boil, reduce the heat, and simmer 1½ hours, or until the beans and lamb are tender. Stir occasionally and make sure there's plenty of water. Add the salt.

3. Heat the oil in a small saucepan over medium low heat. Stir in the flour to make a smooth paste. Add the tomato paste and ½ cup of bean broth, stirring quickly. Simmer, stirring, until the mixture is well thickened, then mix back into the beans. Taste and add more salt and pepper if needed. Cook, stirring occasionally, another

15 to 20 minutes. Just before serving, mix in the lemon juice and cook 1 to 2 minutes more.

SERVES 8 to 10

Boston Baked Beans (with White Beans)

This is Sally Larkin's recipe for Boston baked beans. If desired, a whole peeled onion or two may be placed in the bottom of the pot and one or two sausages may be poked down inside.

3 cups dry small white beans
Cold water to cover beans
4 teaspoons salt
2 teaspoons dry mustard

4 tablespoons firmly packed dark brown sugar
4 tablespoons molasses
¼ pound salt pork

1. Wash and pick over the beans. Soak overnight or for 10 to 12 hours in water to cover (see pages 40–41 for soaking instructions). In the morning bring to boiling point and simmer gently for about 1 hour. Test the beans by blowing on a tablespoonful: When the skins blow off easily, the beans are ready for the pot.
2. Heat the oven to 325°F.
3. Turn the beans into a bean pot. Combine salt, mustard, sugar, and molasses and pour the mixture over the beans. Score the salt pork and place on top. Bake 8 to 10 hours. Check the beans occasionally. Add water if needed. When the beans melt in your mouth, they are done.

SERVES 6 to 8

Baked Beans, Italian Style

Save bits of meat from cooked beef roasts, or a little leftover hamburger to add to the flavor of this dish. It can be served as a side dish or a main course.

2 cups dry small white beans
6 cups cold water
2 teaspoons salt
½ cup olive oil
1 cup cooked beef bits (optional)
1 cup chopped yellow onion
2 medium cloves garlic, peeled
    and minced
1 cup chopped celery
2 tablespoons chopped fresh
    parsley

½ teaspoon dried thyme
¼ teaspoon dried basil
¼ teaspoon black pepper
4 tablespoons tomato paste
1 8-ounce can whole tomatoes
3 tablespoons butter or
    margarine
Grated Parmesan to taste

1. Wash and pick over the beans. Combine the beans with the water and salt in a large kettle, bring to a boil, boil 2 minutes, remove from the heat, cover, and let stand 1 hour. Return to the stove, and cook 2½ hours, or until beans are very tender. Add more water if needed.

2. Heat the oil in a large skillet, and sauté meat bits (if used), onion, garlic, and celery until the onion is translucent. Don't let the vegetables brown. Mix in the remaining ingredients except the butter and cheese. Scrape up the pan juices and cook, stirring, about 5 minutes more. Combine gently with the cooked beans. Turn into a serving casserole, dot with butter, and sprinkle with cheese. Brown under the broiler before serving.

SERVES 6 to 8

French Baked Beans for a Crowd

For a crowd you can use chicken wings instead of lamb shoulder to make a more economical dish. This is a real cassoulet.

4 cups dry small white beans
   Cold water to cover beans
4 ounces salt pork
   Cold water to cover salt pork
1 medium bay leaf
3 sprigs fresh parsley
1 teaspoon dried thyme
4 whole peppercorns
2 carrots, scraped and halved
1 whole yellow onion, peeled
   and stuck with 8 whole cloves
   Salt
1 tablespoon bacon drippings
2 pounds boned pork loin, cubed
   (reserve the bones)

2 pounds boned shoulder lamb,
   cubed (reserve the bones)
2 medium yellow onions, peeled
   and chopped
2 large cloves garlic, peeled and
   minced
1 8-ounce can tomato purée
1 cup beef bouillon
1 large French or hot Italian
   garlic sausage
   Cold water to cover sausage
   Salt and black pepper to taste
1 cup bread crumbs

1. Wash and pick over the beans, place in a large kettle, cover with cold water, and soak overnight (see pages 40–41 for soaking instructions).

2. Next day, in a small saucepan, cover the salt pork with water, bring to a boil, and simmer 5 minutes. Drain and dice.

3. Add the salt pork to the beans and water. Tie up the bay leaf, parsley, thyme, and peppercorns in a small piece of cheesecloth and add to the pot with the carrots, onion stuck with cloves, and 2 teaspoons salt. Over high heat bring to a boil. Reduce the heat, cover and simmer gently for 1 to 1½ hours, or until beans are just tender but still firm. Remove the herb bag, carrots, and onion.

4. While the beans are cooking, prepare the meats. Heat the bacon drippings in a big Dutch oven and brown the pork and lamb cubes and bones. Stir in the chopped onions and garlic and cook 2 minutes. Stir in the tomato purée. Cover and simmer 1 hour, or until the meat is tender. Add beef bouillon as needed if the meat seems to dry out.

5. Prick the sausage all over with a fork. Place in a kettle and cover with water. Bring to a boil and simmer 1 hour. Drain and cut in slices ½ inch thick.

6. Heat oven to 375°F.

7. When the pork and lamb are done, remove the bones. Com-

bine the meat cubes with the cooked beans. Taste and add salt and pepper if necessary. Add more beef bouillon if mixture is dry.

8. In a deep casserole alternate layers of beans-and-meat mixture with sausage slices, ending with a layer of sausage slices. Combine bread crumbs with salt and pepper to taste and sprinkle over the top layer.

9. Bake 1 to 1½ hours. As bread crumbs bake and dry out on top of the casserole, push gently down into the casserole. Serve bubbling hot.

SERVES 12 to 14

Beans Tante Louise

My French aunts prepare *flageolets*, the small dry beans popular in France, by simmering them very slowly with garlic. I cook small white beans the same way. This is easiest to make in a slow cooker: in step 1, place all the ingredients except the salt pork into the cooker and cook on the low-heat setting for 10 to 12 hours or until the beans are tender. Then follow step 2.

2⅔ cups (1 pound) dry small white beans
6 cups cold water
3 large cloves garlic, peeled
1 3-inch piece salt pork
Salt and black pepper to taste

1. Wash and pick over the beans and place them in a large Dutch oven with the cold water. Turn the heat to medium and when the water is boiling, add the garlic, reduce the heat, cover, and simmer, stirring occasionally, until the beans are done. It can take 3 or 4 hours or more, depending on the beans. Check occasionally, and add more cold water if the pot is drying out.

2. When the beans are tender but not breaking up, cut up the salt pork into tiny cubes and sauté in a hot skillet. When the pork has rendered all its fat, remove the rendered pork bits (called *lardons*) with a slotted spoon and stir into the beans. If you wish, stir the fat from the *lardons*, or a little of it, into the beans. Add salt and pepper.

SERVES 6 to 8

Beans and Port

An offbeat variation on Boston baked beans that can also be prepared in a slow cooker: soak the beans before you start (see pages 40–41 for soaking instructions) and cook in the slow cooker on the low-heat setting for 12 to 16 hours, or until beans are tender. Add the port and coffee when the beans are half done.

2⅔ cups (1 pound) dry small white beans	½ teaspoon dry mustard
Cold water to cover beans	½ teaspoon salt
½ pound salt pork cut into ¼-inch-thick slices	½ cup firmly packed light brown sugar
1 medium yellow onion, peeled and chopped	1½ cups cooking port
	1 cup strong coffee

1. Soak the beans in cold water to cover overnight.
2. Heat the oven to 275°F.
3. In a large Dutch oven or a heavy kettle over medium heat cook the salt pork and onion until the onion is translucent, 5 to 10 minutes. Add the drained beans (reserve the liquid), mustard, salt, sugar, 1 cup port, and just enough of the soaking liquid to cover the beans. Scrape up the pan juices. Cover and bake for about 4 hours. Check occasionally and if the dish is drying out, add more of the soaking water. After 4 hours add the remaining port and the coffee, and bake another 1½ to 2 hours.

SERVES 6 to 8

Michigan-Style Creamed Beans

Cooking water left over from bean dishes can be frozen and used for cooking a bean soup.

2 cups dry small white beans	1½ teaspoons salt
Warm water to cover beans	½ teaspoon black pepper
⅓ teaspoon ground ginger	1 tablespoon light molasses
2 large yellow onions, peeled and chopped	1 cup boiling bean liquid
⅓ cup sour cream	2 to 3 tablespoons butter or margarine

1. Place the beans in a medium kettle, add enough warm water to cover, and soak overnight (see pages 40–41 for soaking instructions). In the same water, over medium-high heat, bring the beans to a boil, add the ginger, cover, and cook until the beans are becoming tender and skins are breaking, about 2 hours. Stir the beans now and then; you may need to add more water. Drain the beans, reserving the liquid. Combine the onions with the beans in the pot and turn the mixture into a 1½- to 2-quart casserole that has a lid.

2. Heat the oven to 350°F.

3. In a small bowl mix together the sour cream, salt, pepper, and molasses. Pour this over the beans and add 1 cup of boiling bean liquid. Cover and bake 2 hours. Turn the heat to 375°F., uncover the casserole, dot with butter or margarine, and bake until the top is brown, another 20 to 30 minutes.

SERVES 6

Beans and Short Ribs of Beef

Short ribs can be a good buy, especially when they are thick and meaty. This is an easy way to cook them with baked-in beans. The small white beans are slow to cook, and the overnight soak is often recommended for them (see pages 40–41 for soaking instructions).

1⅓ cups (½ pound) dry small white beans	3 large yellow onions, peeled and chopped
1 quart cold water	1 large clove garlic, peeled and minced
1 tablespoon butter or margarine	2 cups celery, sliced into ½-inch-thick pieces
2 pounds short ribs of beef, cut into 2-inch pieces	3 tablespoons tomato paste
½ teaspoon salt	2 tablespoons minced fresh parsley
¼ teaspoon black pepper	

1. Wash and pick over the beans and soak them overnight or for 10 to 12 hours in the water. Drain the beans, reserving the

soaking water. Heat 3 cups of the soaking water, add the beans, bring to a boil, then reduce the heat, cover, and simmer.

2. While the beans are cooking, melt the butter or margarine in a large Dutch oven or a heavy kettle and brown the short ribs over medium heat. Add salt and pepper. Turn often. Toward the end add the onions, garlic, and celery and stir together. Cook another 5 minutes, then add the beans and cooking liquid. Scrape up the juices in the bottom of the pan, stir in the tomato paste, cover and cook over low heat for 2½ to 3 hours, or until meat and beans are very tender. Stir occasionally and add more water as needed. Before serving taste and add more salt and pepper if desired. Garnish with parsley.

SERVES 6

Baked Beef and Beans

A meaty dish sauced with tomatoes and spiced a little by a teaspoon of chili powder. It tastes best when you have roast drippings to add—but you can use lard instead.

1 cup dry small white beans
6 cups cold water
*2 tablespoons all-purpose
    flour*
1½ teaspoons salt
*1 pound stew beef, cut into
    1-inch pieces*

*2 tablespoons drippings from
    pork or beef roast, or 2
    tablespoons lard*
1 8-ounce can tomato sauce
*3 small yellow onions, peeled and
    halved*
1 teaspoon chili powder

1. Wash and pick over the beans. Combine the beans with the water in a saucepan, bring to a boil, boil 2 minutes, remove from the heat, cover, and let stand 2 hours.

2. Heat the oven to 325°F.

3. Combine the flour and salt and coat the beef pieces with the mixture. Place a medium Dutch oven or kettle over medium heat and melt the drippings in it. Brown the beef pieces thoroughly. Add the tomato sauce, scraping up the bottom of the pan to get all the drippings. Add the onions and stir in the chili powder. Drain

the beans, reserving the liquid, and measure out 2 cups of bean liquid. Mix the beans into the meat and add the 2 cups bean liquid. Cover and bake 2½ hours, or until meat and beans are done. Stir now and then, and if needed, add reserved bean liquid.

SERVES 4 to 5

Lamb and Bean Stew

2⅔ cups (1 pound) dry small
    white beans
6 cups cold water
1 cup chopped yellow onion
2 tablespoons olive or
    vegetable oil
1½ pounds boneless stew lamb,
    cut into 1-inch cubes
1 bay leaf
1 teaspoon oregano
1 teaspoon dried thyme

1 teaspoon dried rosemary
2 medium cloves garlic, peeled
    and minced
2 teaspoons salt
½ teaspoon black pepper
1 cup peeled, seeded, and diced
    fresh tomatoes
¼ cup minced fresh parsley
4 tablespoons butter or margarine
    at room temperature
Salt and black pepper to taste

1. Wash and pick over the beans. Combine with the water in a large kettle, bring to a boil, reduce the heat, and boil 2 minutes; remove from the heat, cover, and let stand 1 hour. Return to the heat and simmer 1½ hours.

2. Simmer the onion in the oil in a Dutch oven or a large heavy kettle over medium heat until the onion is translucent. Push the onion to one side and brown the lamb cubes in the skillet. Drain the beans, reserving the liquid. Add the beans and 1½ cups of bean liquid to the Dutch oven. If necessary, add enough more water to make 1½ cups liquid. Add the seasonings, scrape up the meat cooking juices from the bottom of the pot, cover, and cook over low heat 1 hour. Add the tomatoes, cover, and cook about 30 minutes longer, or until beans and lamb are tender. Mash the parsley into the butter or margarine. Just before serving, spread the parsley butter over the lamb and beans. Add more salt and pepper to taste.

SERVES 6 to 8

Beans, Macaroni, and Sausage Casserole

2⅔ cups (1 pound) dry small
    white beans
6 cups cold water
2 tablespoons vegetable oil
1 pound fresh pork sausage
1 large clove garlic, peeled
    and minced
1 16-ounce can whole tomatoes

¾ cup dark corn syrup
2 tablespoons fresh chopped basil
    or 1 tablespoon dried basil
1 teaspoon salt
1 teaspoon dried oregano
¼ teaspoon black pepper
1 8-ounce package elbow
    macaroni, cooked

1. Wash and pick over the beans. Combine the beans with the water in a large kettle, bring to a boil, boil 2 minutes, remove from the heat, cover, and let stand 1 hour.

2. Return beans to the heat, bring to a boil, and simmer 2 hours, or until the beans are tender. Drain, reserving the cooking liquid.

3. Heat the oil in a large, deep skillet and brown the sausage and the garlic. Break the sausage into bits and cook until it is all crispy brown, about 15 minutes. Add the tomatoes, corn syrup, 1 cup of the bean liquid, basil, salt, oregano, and pepper. Break up the tomatos and mix skillet contents well. Cover, reduce heat, and simmer 15 minutes. Stir in the beans and cooked macaroni, cover, and simmer 15 minutes more over medium-low heat.

SERVES 6 to 8

11

Light and Dark Red Kidney Beans

The red kidney beans have a strong nutty flavor and, like pink beans, are often used in Mexican and Latin American cooking. They can replace pink or pinto beans in any of the Mexican dishes, while the pinks or pintos can be used successfully in the Latin American dishes in this chapter. Chances are that in the supermarket you'll find other red beans—small reds with Latin brand names and big light reds. These can be used instead of the kidney beans but aren't as attractive in salads. They also take longer to cook.

Since the dark red kidney beans are slower to cook than the light reds, they are the ones used most often in commercial cooking. The light red kidney beans are those most often used in home recipes calling for simply "red kidney beans." But the flavor of both is generally similar, and they can be used interchangeably.

Red kidney beans are especially popular in salads. They stand up particularly well to cooking, don't seem to disintegrate as easily as the pinks and pintos, and add interesting color to the dishes in which they are used. They go well with fruit and strong salad dressings—Sweet and Sour Kidney Beans with Pears (page 129), for instance—and are also great in soups. I've included here Kidney Bean Soup with Red Wine (page 121), and Kidney Bean and Ginger Soup (pages 121–122), both of which are a bit different from the usual bean soups.

Kidney Bean Soup with Red Wine

This is made with red wine and has an herb flavor that is dry and rather special. Serve it with crusty French bread.

1⅓ cups (½ pound) dry light
    red kidney beans
4 cups cold water
1 tablespoon salt
3 tablespoons butter or
    margarine
¾ cup chopped yellow onion

½ cup grated carrot
1 cup chopped celery
1 teaspoon dried marjoram
⅛ teaspoon black pepper
1 cup dry red wine
2 tablespoons butter

1. Wash and pick over the beans. Combine the beans with the cold water in a saucepan, bring to a boil, boil 2 minutes, remove from the heat, cover, and let stand 1 hour. Return to the heat and simmer 2 hours, or until the beans are very tender. Check and add more water if water level falls, since the bean water and the wine are the only liquids in this soup. Add the salt.

2. Melt 2 tablespoons butter or margarine in a large skillet and sauté the onion, carrot, and celery until the onion is translucent. Do not allow the onion to brown. Add the marjoram, pepper, and wine; heat briefly, then stir into the beans. Purée the mixture a cupful at a time in the blender at medium speed. Make sure liquid is added to the blender each time. When all is done, return the soup to the saucepan and heat thoroughly. Serve with a dab of butter in each plate.

SERVES 4 to 6

Kidney Bean and Ginger Soup

This soup can be prepared in a slow cooker by starting with step 2, using 5 cups of water instead of 6, and cooking on the low-heat setting for 10 to 12 hours, or until the beans are tender.

1 cup dry light red kidney beans
6 cups cold water
5 tablespoons butter or margarine
1 medium yellow onion, peeled
  and minced
1 medium clove garlic, peeled
  and minced
2 stalks celery, minced

½ teaspoon ground sage
½ teaspoon ground ginger
1 tablespoon catsup
1 teaspoon salt
⅛ teaspoon black pepper
4 slices stale white bread, crusts
  removed, cubed
2 tablespoons chopped fresh mint

1. Wash the beans and pick them over. Combine the beans with water in a saucepan, bring to a boil, boil 2 minutes, remove from the heat, cover, and let stand 1 hour.

2. Heat 2 tablespoons butter or margarine in a small saucepan and sauté the onion, garlic, and celery over medium heat until the onion is translucent, 5 to 7 minutes. Scrape into the beans. Add the sage and ginger, then cover and simmer until the beans are very tender, about 2 hours. Add the catsup, salt, and pepper and mash the beans and mix them into the liquid. Or, a little at a time, blend beans and cooking liquid in the blender, then return to the soup. Heat to the boiling point, then remove from the heat.

3. In a skillet, melt 3 tablespoons butter over medium heat and sauté the bread cubes until golden and crisp. Serve sprinkled over the hot soup. Garnish with chopped mint.

SERVES 4

Kidney Bean and Lamb Soup

1 *cup dry light red kidney beans*
  Cold water to cover beans
2 *tablespoons butter or margarine*
1 *large lamb shank*
1 *large yellow onion, peeled and*
  chopped
1 *medium clove garlic, peeled*
  and minced
1 *large stalk celery, with leaves,*
  minced
1 *medium carrot, scraped and*
  diced

1 *small bay leaf*
1½ *teaspoon salt*
¼ *teaspoon ground cloves*
¼ *teaspoon dried thyme*
  Hot water
1 *cup tomato juice*
2 *teaspoons strained lemon*
  juice
  Salt and black pepper to taste

1. Wash and pick over the beans, cover with cold water, bring to a boil, boil 2 minutes, then remove from the heat, cover, and let soak 1 hour.

2. Heat the oven to 300°F.

3. Melt the butter or margarine in a large Dutch oven or a big kettle and brown the lamb shank over medium-high heat until dark golden all over. Add the onion and garlic and continue to brown until the onion is translucent. Add the celery, carrot, and seasonings, and cook another 3 or 4 minutes, stirring. Measure the bean cooking liquid, and add enough hot water to make 1½ quarts. Add this liquid, along with the beans and tomato juice, to the lamb shank. Scrape the bottom of the pot to get up the browned bits, then cover and bake 2 hours. Remove the lamb shank from the pot, remove the meat from the bone, dice it, and add the diced meat and the lemon juice to the soup. Discard the bone. Add pepper and more salt to taste. Heat well just before serving.

SERVES 6

Orange Wedges and Kidney Bean Salad

This dish tastes best when the oranges and beans have a chance to marinate in the tart French dressing before it is served, so try to prepare it in advance. Orange wedges are orange sections with the membranes removed.

2 cups canned or cooked dark   1 teaspoon salt
    red kidney beans, drained   ¼ teaspoon granulated sugar
1 can mandarin oranges,   ⅛ teaspoon black pepper
    drained, or 1 cup fresh   ⅛ teaspoon dry mustard
    orange wedges   Iceberg lettuce cups
6 tablespoons vegetable oil
1½ tablespoons wine vinegar

1. Combine the drained beans and mandarin oranges or the fresh orange wedges in a large bowl, toss well. Reserve a few orange sections for garnish.

2. Combine the remaining ingredients except the lettuce in the blender and blend a minute or so at a low speed. Pour the dressing over the bean mixture and toss together. Serve in crisp lettuce cups and garnish with reserved orange wedges.

SERVES 4 to 6

Kidney Bean Salad with Yogurt Dressing

Salads are the ideal way to use leftover cooked beans. This one has a sweet-and-sour flavor. It's a great picnic or cook-out dish. Make it ahead of time and allow the ingredients to marinate a little in the sauce.

2 cups cooked or canned dark   Salt
    red kidney beans, drained   2 teaspoons granulated sugar
2 hardboiled eggs, chopped   2 teaspoons red wine vinegar
½ cup chopped celery   ½ teaspoon dry mustard
¼ cup chopped sweet pickle   ½ teaspoon soy sauce
¼ cup chopped cucumber,   ½ cup plain yogurt
    including rind   ⅛ teaspoon paprika

1. Combine beans, eggs, celery, pickle, and cucumber in a large salad bowl. Sprinkle with ½ teaspoon salt and toss carefully so the egg doesn't disintegrate.

2. Mix ½ teaspoon salt and remaining ingredients in a small bowl. Combine the two mixtures, taste, and add more salt and more soy sauce, if desired. Cover and chill a few hours before serving.

SERVES 4 to 6

Crunchy Kidney Bean Salad

This dish is flavored with mustard relish and curry and is made crunchy by the addition of chopped celery and onion.

2 cups cooked or canned light red kidney beans, drained
1 medium yellow onion, peeled and diced
3 medium stalks of celery, diced (leaves removed)

¼ cup mayonnaise
¼ cup mustard relish
1 teaspoon curry powder
⅛ teaspoon white pepper
2 hardboiled eggs, peeled

1. Turn the beans into a large mixing bowl and add the onion and celery. In a small bowl combine the mayonnaise, mustard relish, curry powder, and white pepper. Taste and add more curry powder if you wish. Combine thoroughly with the vegetables. Cover and chill.

2. Just before serving, slice eggs and toss gently into the salad.

SERVES 4 to 6

Kidney Bean and Basil Salad

A hearty salad that can be lunch all by itself: Serve with hot bread and butter, cheese, and a dessert.

1 cup cooked or canned light red kidney beans, drained
1 medium Spanish onion, peeled and chopped
2 large ripe tomatoes, chopped
1 medium cucumber, peeled and chopped
½ cup minced parsley

1 tablespoon fresh basil or ½ tablespoon dried basil
¼ cup vegetable oil
⅛ cup strained lemon juice
2 tablespoons red wine vinegar
½ teaspoon salt
⅛ teaspoon black pepper
Iceberg lettuce cups

Combine the vegetables. Blend the parsley and remaining ingredients except the lettuce in a blender at medium speed and pour over the vegetables. Taste and correct seasoning if needed. Toss the vegetables in the dressing. Cover and chill for several hours. Serve in individual lettuce cups.

SERVES 4

Kidney Bean and Lentil Salad

Lentils are little flattish brown legumes, like tiny dry split peas. They have a meaty flavor that combines very well with light red kidney beans.

2 cups cooked or canned light
     red kidney beans, drained
1 cup lentils, cooked according
     to package instructions
     and drained
1 medium yellow onion, peeled
     and chopped
½ cup chopped green pepper
1 medium stalk celery, with
     leaves, chopped

½ carrot, peeled and grated
2 tablespoons minced parsley
1 cup mayonnaise
2½ teaspoons white wine vinegar
1 tablespoon catsup
½ teaspoon prepared mustard
1 teaspoon soy sauce
   Salt and black pepper to taste

In a large bowl combine beans and lentils with onion, pepper, celery, and carrot. Mix remaining ingredients in a small bowl. Pour over the vegetables and toss thoroughly. Taste and add salt and pepper if desired.

SERVES 4 to 6

Kidney Beans, Wheat Germ, and Bourbon

The wheat germ here is wholesome but optional. It can be replaced with 1 cup of cooked brown rice.

4 cups cooked or canned dark
  red kidney beans
1 medium yellow onion, peeled
  and chopped
2 tablespoons wheat germ or 1
  cup cooked brown rice
1 large tart apple, cored, peeled,
  and chopped
½ tablespoon lemon juice,
  strained
3 tablespoons bourbon, rum,
  or sherry

1 tablespoon light molasses
1 large clove garlic, peeled
  and minced
1 teaspoon dry mustard
1 teaspoon salt
¼ teaspoon black pepper
⅛ teaspoon ground cloves
1 small bay leaf
⅛ teaspoon ground thyme
⅛ teaspoon ground marjoram
3 to 4 drops hot pepper sauce
6 thick slices bacon (optional)

1. Heat the oven to 350°F.

2. Drain the beans and reserve ½ cup of the liquid. (If there is less, mix in bouillon, using boiling water and a bouillon beef cube to make ½ cup.) In a 1½- or 2-quart casserole that has a cover, layer the beans, onion, and wheat germ. Toss the apple with the lemon juice and sprinkle over the last layer. Combine the reserved bean liquid with bourbon, molasses and all the seasonings and pour over the casserole contents. Lay the bacon strips on top, cover, and bake 1 hour. Reduce the temperature to 300°F. and bake 1 hour more.

SERVES 6

Western-Style Kidney Beans

Here we start with dry beans. This dish can be prepared in a slow cooker starting at step 3: Cook on the low-heat setting for about 4 to 6 hours, or until the beans are tender.

2⅔ cups (1 pound) dry light red   ½ cup dark corn syrup
    kidney beans   ⅓ cup catsup
 5 cups water   2 teaspoons salt
 1 16-ounce can whole tomatoes   1 tablespoon dry mustard
 6 slices bacon   1 large clove garlic, peeled
 2 large tart apples, cored,   and minced
    pared, and chopped   Salt and black pepper to taste
 1 large yellow onion, peeled
    and chopped

1. Wash and pick over the beans. Combine beans with the water in a saucepan, bring to a boil, boil 2 minutes, remove from the heat, cover, and let stand 1 hour. Return to the heat, bring to a boil, and cook about 1 hour, or until beans are just tender. Check occasionally and add more water if beans are drying out. Drain, reserving 1 cup of the cooking liquid.

2. Heat the oven to 300°F.

3. In a 2½-quart casserole, combine beans, the bean liquid, and all remaining ingredients. Place a lid over ⅘ of the casserole top (so that some steam escapes) and bake 2 hours. Remove lid and bake 1 hour longer, uncovered, so that the sauce thickens. Add pepper and more salt to taste.

SERVES 6 to 8

Red Cabbage, Red Beans, and White Wine

In late summer, when red cabbage is plentiful, save a half or quarter of a cabbage to try this. If you have no white wine, use red wine vinegar or cider vinegar.

3 tablespoons butter or margarine   ⅛ teaspoon black pepper
3 tablespoons minced yellow onion   4 tablespoons dry white wine
4 cups shredded red cabbage   2 tablespoons white wine
4 tablespoons light brown sugar,   vinegar
    firmly packed   1½ cups cooked or canned dark
1 teaspoon salt   red kidney beans, drained

Melt the butter or margarine in a very large skillet over medium heat, and in it sauté the onion and shredded cabbage until cabbage begins to wilt, 3 or 4 minutes. Combine brown sugar, salt, and pepper with the wine and vinegar, pour over the cabbage, and mix well. Stir in the beans, cover, and cook for 30 to 40 minutes over medium-low heat, just high enough to keep the contents simmering. Stir occasionally. If the dish dries out, add a little warm water.

SERVES 4

Sweet-and-Sour Kidney Beans and Pears

A sweet-and-sour dish to serve with roast ham or pork—unusual and delightful.

2 cups cooked or canned light red kidney beans	1 teaspoon grated orange rind
5 tablespoons firmly packed light brown sugar	1 16-ounce can pear halves
1 tablespoon white vinegar	2 firmly packed tablespoons light brown sugar
1 tablespoon yellow onion, peeled and minced	1½ teaspoons prepared mustard
	½ teaspoon ground cloves

1. Combine the beans and bean liquid, 3 tablespoons of the brown sugar, vinegar, onion, and orange rind in a 1½-quart casserole. Drain the pears, reserving 2 tablespoons of the syrup, and arrange the pear halves over the beans.
2. Heat the oven to 350°F.
3. Mix 2 tablespoons pear syrup, 2 more tablespoons brown sugar, mustard, and cloves in a small bowl and spoon over the pears. Cover and bake 25 or 30 minutes.

SERVES 4 to 6

Kidney Beans, Artichoke Hearts, and Onion Rings

This dish has a robust flavor and is delicious served with grilled meats and hot bread.

4 cups cooked or canned light
     red kidney beans, drained
2 6-ounce jars marinated
     artichoke hearts, drained
1 cup minced celery
½ cup minced yellow onion
1 cup vegetable oil
¼ cup red wine vinegar

2 teaspoons salt
½ teaspoon granulated sugar
¼ teaspoon dry mustard
¼ teaspoon black pepper
1 medium Spanish or red onion,
     peeled and sliced thin
8 to 12 red radishes, sliced

1. Turn the beans into a large mixing bowl and combine with the artichoke hearts, celery, and minced onion.

2. Combine the oil, vinegar, salt, sugar, mustard, and pepper in the blender at medium speed. Pour over the bean mixture and toss well together. Cover and chill for several hours.

3. Before serving, drain off excess dressing, turn bean mixture into a salad bowl, and garnish with thin slices of Spanish onion and radish slices.

SERVES 6 to 8

Kidney Beans and Spareribs

This is a casserole from the Caribbean, simple to put together, takes a while to cook, and is delicious to eat.

1½ cups dry light red kidney beans
4½ cups cold water
1 tablespoon vegetable oil
¼ pound chorizo, or hot Italian
     sausage, sliced into ¼-
     inch-thick pieces

1 pound spareribs, in 1-rib
     pieces
1 cup medium dry Madeira
     wine

1. Wash and pick over the beans. Combine them with the water in a saucepan, bring to a boil, boil 2 minutes, remove from the heat, cover, and let stand 1 hour.

2. Add the oil to the beans, bring to a boil, and simmer 1 to 2 hours, or until the beans are barely tender. Check periodically and add more water if the beans are drying out.

3. Heat the oven to 350°F.

4. Scrape ⅓ of the beans into a 4-quart casserole. Sprinkle ½ of the sausage meat over the beans and cover with ½ of the spareribs. Repeat the layers and end with a third layer of beans. Pour the Madeira over the top, cover, and bake 1 hour. Uncover and continue baking about 1 hour longer, or until the sauce is very thick and the ribs are tender. Skim away excess fat from the top of the casserole before serving.

SERVES 4

Diced Ham and Red Kidney Beans

1 tablespoon vegetable oil
1 cup chopped yellow onion
1 cup chopped, seeded, green
* pepper*
2 tablespoons red wine vinegar
1 tablespoon cornstarch
3 tablespoons tomato paste
2 tablespoons firmly packed light
* brown sugar*
¼ teaspoon ground thyme
1 tablespoon Worcestershire
* sauce*
½ teaspoon dry mustard
4 cups cooked or canned dark
* red kidney beans and liquid*
2 cups diced cooked ham

1. Heat the oven to 350°F.
2. Heat the oil in a large skillet over medium heat and sauté the onion and pepper until the onion is translucent. Mix together the vinegar, cornstarch, tomato paste, brown sugar, thyme, Worcestershire sauce, and mustard and stir into the kidney beans. Turn into the skillet and combine well. Add the ham, toss together, then turn the skillet contents into a 1½- or 2-quart baking dish. Cover and bake 30 minutes. If the dish dries, add a little tomato paste mixed with water to moisten it.

SERVES 4 to 6

Kidney Beans and Bread, Italian Style

This is one of my favorite ways of using up those lovely slices of French or Italian bread that are left over from other dinner parties. The recipe begins with dry beans, but you can use cooked or canned beans, and start the recipe at step 2.

2⅔ cups dark red kidney beans
    Water to cover beans
¼ pound salt pork
1 large clove garlic, peeled
    and minced
8 sprigs fresh parsley
2 teaspoons salt
½ teaspoon dried oregano
½ teaspoon dried basil

¼ teaspoon black pepper
1 16-ounce can Italian plum
    tomatoes
1 large loaf Italian bread or
    20 slices stale French or
    Italian bread
½ pound mozzarella cheese,
    grated
3 cups grated Parmesan cheese

1. Wash and pick over the beans, cover with water, bring to a boil, boil 2 minutes, remove from the heat, cover and let stand 1 hour. Return to the heat and simmer 1½ hours.

2. Slice the salt pork into shreds, chop into it the garlic and parsley, and mix well with the salt, oregano, basil, and pepper. When the beans have cooked 1½ hours, add the salt pork mixture to the beans along with the tomatoes. Stir together, cover, and simmer 30 more minutes, stirring occasionally.

3. Cut the bread into 20 1-inch slices and dry out in a slow (325°F.) oven. Put 2 slices of bread on each plate. Top with 3 tablespoons mozzarella cheese, then 1 cup of the bean mixture. Garnish with Parmesan cheese and pass under a hot broiler 2 minutes.

SERVES 10

Kidney Beans with Burgundy

This is a West Coast recipe made with Monterey Jack cheese, but Cheddar or cream cheese will work just as well.

2⅔ cups (1 pound) dry light
    red kidney beans
5 cups cold water
1 tablespoon vegetable oil
⅔ pound ground beef
2 teaspoons chili powder
1 16-ounce can whole tomatoes

1 cup Burgundy
½ cup chopped yellow onion
1 large clove garlic, peeled and
    minced
2 teaspoons salt
½ pound Monterey Jack or
    Cheddar cheese, diced

1. Wash and pick over the beans. Combine the beans with the water in a saucepan, heat to boiling, boil 2 minutes, cover, and remove from the heat. Let stand 1 hour, then return to the heat and cook 1 hour longer. If the beans seem dry, add a little more water.

2. Heat the oil in a large saucepan over medium high heat, add the meat, and stir and cook until the meat is well crumbled and brown all over. Mix in the chili powder a few minutes before the meat is completely browned.

3. Mix the meat into the beans with the remaining ingredients except the cheese and simmer, covered, for another 30 minutes. If the beans still contain much liquid, do not cover the saucepan. Shortly before the cooking period is over, gently mix in the cheese, and let simmer another few minutes. Do not stir until the cheese has all melted.

SERVES 8

New York Chili and Beans

This is a variation on Mexican chili. The sauce tastes more Italian than Mexican. It is thinned with beer and served with minced onion on the side and crackers. It makes good use of leftover bacon drippings.

½ cup bacon drippings	⅛ teaspoon dried oregano
2 pounds ground beef	⅛ teaspoon black pepper
1 cup chopped yellow onion	⅛ teaspoon crushed red pepper
1 cup chopped green pepper	2 17-ounce cans whole
1 large clove garlic, peeled	tomatoes
and minced	1 6-ounce can tomato paste
5 tablespoons chili powder	6 to 8 cups cooked or canned
1 tablespoon salt	dark red kidney beans
2 teaspoons ground cumin	Beer
1½ teaspoons dry mustard	

Heat the bacon drippings in a large skillet or kettle over medium heat and sauté the meat, stirring to break it into bits. Brown it well.

Add the onion, pepper, seasonings, and tomatoes; mix well, reduce the heat, and cook for about 1½ hours. Add the tomato paste and the beans and continue cooking another hour. Stir occasionally, and as the liquid thickens, thin with a little beer.

SERVES 8 to 10

Beans with Mexican Chili Sauce for a Crowd

The ½ cup of chili powder called for makes a chili that I find hot; if you prefer milder chili, use ¼ cup. Chopped onion and crushed red pepper are good garnishes to offer in small side dishes.

3 tablespoons vegetable oil
8 medium yellow onions, peeled and chopped
5 pounds ground beef chuck
20 medium cloves garlic, peeled and minced
½ cup chili powder (or less to taste)
1 tablespoon ground cumin
1 tablespoon dried oregano
⅛ teaspoon ground cloves

2 stalks celery, with leaves, minced
1 tablespoon salt
¼ teaspoon black pepper
6½ cups (about 2 28-ounce cans) canned whole tomatoes, drained
6 tablespoons tomato paste
7 to 10 cups cooked or canned dark red kidney beans with liquid

1. Heat the oil in a very large skillet or kettle and add the onions. Cook over medium heat, stirring, until the onions are translucent, 6 to 8 minutes. Add the meat and continue to cook, stirring to break the meat into bits. Brown well all over. Add the garlic, chili powder, cumin, oregano, cloves, and celery and stir and cook for 3 to 4 minutes. Add the salt and pepper. Combine tomatoes and tomato paste and stir into the sauce. Taste and add a little more salt and pepper if desired. Cook, stirring occasionally, about 1 hour. If the sauce dries out, add a little beef bouillon. Turn into a serving dish.
2. Heat the beans in the cooking or canning liquid, drain well, and serve in a separate dish.

SERVES 15 to 20

Spanish Rice with Red Kidney Beans

A quick and easy way to put together a hearty, inexpensive meatless casserole or side dish.

1 5½-ounce package Uncle Ben's Spanish rice
1 cup cooked or canned red kidney beans, drained
1 teaspoon canned green chilis (optional)

2 tablespoons olive or vegetable oil
1 medium clove garlic, peeled and minced

Cook the Spanish rice, following package instructions. Mix in the beans, and the chilis if used. In a small saucepan warm the oil and sauté the garlic until lightly browned. Strain out the garlic bits and mix the oil into the rice dish.

SERVES 4 to 6

Kidney Beans and Mock Cornmeal Dumplings

To get the dumplings just right in this recipe, be sure the casserole contents are bubbling hot before you drop the cornbread into it.

1 1½-ounce envelope enchilada sauce mix
1 8-ounce can tomato sauce
1½ cups cold water
1 tablespoon vegetable oil

½ pound ground beef
3 cups cooked or canned light red kidney beans, drained
1 small package cornbread mix

1. Follow package directions to make the enchilada sauce, using the tomato sauce and 1½ cups of water.
2. While the sauce simmers, heat the oil in a medium skillet over medium-high heat, add the ground beef, and stir and turn the meat until it is well browned all over and crumbled. Stir a little of the enchilada sauce into the skillet, scrape up the pan juices, turn off the heat, and scrape the skillet contents into the sauce.
3. Heat the oven to 375°F.

4. Empty the beans into a 1½-quart casserole, stir in the enchilada sauce and meat, cover, and set in the oven. While the sauce heats to bubbling, mix the cornbread, following package instructions. (Measure the liquid for the mix carefully and skimp on it a little.) When the sauce is bubbling, drop the cornbread mix by the spoonful over the top until the top is crowned with dumplings. Put any remaining batter into a small, greased pie plate, and set the plate in the oven. Bake 20 to 25 minutes, or until cornbread dumplings are done and cornbread is cooked. Serve together.

SERVES 6

12

Blackeyes and Yellow Eyes

The recipes in this chapter are for blackeyes, but you can use yellow eyes instead if yellow eyes grow best in your area. Blackeyes are the West's equivalent of yellow eyes, which are a southern shell bean. A number of these recipes are adaptations of old southern dishes.

Blackeye Cream Soup (pages 138–139), made with pork hocks, is a southern dish, great as a one-dish dinner. Blackeye Hash (page 148) is considered "soul" food, as is Shrimp Creole with Blackeyes (page 143). Dry Blackeyes, Southern Style (page 141) is a classic way to prepare the beans with salt pork, onions, garlic, and celery. Blackeye Chili (page 146) and Blackeyes, Brazilian Style (pages 144–145) are both Latin dishes.

Blackeyes are different from the common shell bean. They cook more quickly, are less mealy, and have a different flavor—less nutty, more like snap beans, to my mind—from most shell beans.

The shelled beans are very good fresh, and that's the way they are used in the South. But when the fresh yellow-eye bean season has gone by, Southerners import blackeyes from California. They are a big commercial crop there.

Blackeye Dip

A great way to use leftover blackeyes. It's good with celery sticks or apple slices and makes a nice sandwich spread on brown bread.

1 cup cooked or canned
   blackeyes, drained
½ pint sour cream
2 tablespoons minced or mashed
   yellow onion

2 tablespoons minced green pepper
   or minced canned pimiento
1 dash Tabasco sauce (optional)
   Salt and black pepper (optional)

Mash the blackeyes in a medium bowl, then beat in the remaining ingredients except salt and pepper. Taste and add salt and pepper if you think they are needed.

YIELDS 2 cups

Blackeye Cream Soup

A really meaty soup that makes a great one-dish dinner.

2 cups dry blackeye beans
8 cups water
3 ham hocks
½ cup chopped yellow onion
3 cups celery, with leaves,
   chopped
3 small carrots, scraped and
   sliced in thin rounds

3 tablespoons chili powder
2 cups beef bouillon
1 cup light cream or half-
   and-half
1 pound Polish sausage, sliced
   very thin
1 teaspoon salt
⅛ teaspoon black pepper

1. Wash and pick over the beans. Place in a large saucepan with the water and bring to a boil.

2. Add the ham hocks, onion, celery, and carrots. Cook, covered, for 2 to 3 hours, or until the meat is falling off the bones. Remove the ham hocks, mince the meat, and discard the bones.

3. Drain the vegetables, reserving the cooking liquid, and press through a food mill, or blend in the blender with a little of the cooking liquid. Return ham and vegetables to the saucepan, add the

remaining ingredients, and simmer, covered, for another 30 minutes. Add more seasoning if desired.

SERVES 6 to 8

Marinated Blackeye and Rice Salad

This is a great dish to put together the day before a party. The flavor is best when the beans and the rice are mixed with the dressing while they are still warm.

5 cups cooked or canned
   blackeye beans
1 cup vegetable oil
1/8 cup cider vinegar
1 teaspoon salt
1/2 teaspoon granulated sugar
1/4 teaspoon dry mustard
1/8 teaspoon black pepper
3 cups hot, cooked, converted
   white rice

3/4 cup chopped yellow onion
3/4 cup chopped celery
3/4 cup grated raw carrot
1/2 cup diced green pepper
1/3 cup diced pimiento
1 cup diced cooked ham
   Lettuce cups

1. If you've just cooked the beans, drain them. If you are starting with cold beans, warm them in their liquid, then drain them. In the blender blend the oil with the vinegar, salt, sugar, mustard, and pepper. Add ⅔ of this mixture to beans, combine well, cool to room temperature, then cover and chill.

2. Add the remaining dressing to the rice while still hot and mix well. Cool, then cover and chill.

3. Several hours before serving, combine beans, rice, and the remaining ingredients except lettuce cups. Cover and chill until ready to serve. Serve in lettuce cups.

SERVES 10,

Blackeyes in Lettuce Cups with Blue Cheese Dressing

Nifty as a luncheon or dinner salad that goes well with hamburgers or steak. Add salt and blue cheese to your own taste.

Iceberg lettuce

1 red apple

2 tablespoons strained lemon
   juice

½ cup vegetable oil

3 tablespoons wine vinegar

½ teaspoon dry mustard

½ teaspoon granulated sugar

2 to 3 teaspoons salt

⅛ teaspoon black pepper

1 medium clove garlic, peeled
   and crushed

2 to 4 ounces blue cheese or
   Roquefort cheese

4 cups cooked or canned
   blackeye peas, drained

1. Wash the lettuce and separate the leaves. Wash and core the apple and cut into thin slices, unpeeled; toss slices in lemon juice so they won't brown.

2. Combine oil and all remaining ingredients except beans in a bowl, and with a fork beat ingredients together. The blue cheese is nicer if crumbled rather than blended.

3. Combine dressing and beans, then spoon onto lettuce leaves and garnish with apple slices.

SERVES 4 to 6

Turkey Salad with Blackeyes

A new and interesting way to use leftover turkey meat; especially nice with corn bread.

4 cups cooked or canned
   blackeye beans, drained

1 cup shredded celery

1 cup chopped yellow onion

1 cup diced green pepper

¼ cup diced pimiento

1 cup vegetable oil

⅛ cup cider vinegar

½ teaspoon granulated sugar

1 teaspoon salt

¼ teaspoon dry mustard

⅛ teaspoon black pepper

2 cups cooked, diced turkey

1 cup mayonnaise

⅛ teaspoon prepared mustard

½ teaspoon lemon juice

1 small head iceberg lettuce,
   shredded

Combine the beans and vegetables in a large bowl. In the blender blend together the oil, vinegar, sugar, salt, dry mustard, and pepper. Taste and add more salt if you wish. Pour the mixture over the vegetables and toss well. Mix in the turkey. Make a dressing by combining the mayonnaise, prepared mustard, and lemon juice. Serve Turkey Salad on shredded lettuce with dressing on the side.

SERVES 6 to 8

Dry Blackeyes, Southern Style

A dish of the Old South, this takes about three hours to cook. Make the entire amount—2 pounds (5 to 6 cups) of dry beans— and freeze in lots big enough to serve your family (see pages 26–29). You can also prepare this dish in a slow cooker by using only twice as much water as there are beans, and cooking 8 to 10 hours (or until beans are tender) on the low-heat setting.

2 *pounds dry blackeyes*
4 *quarts cold water*
⅔ *pound salt pork*
1 *large yellow onion, peeled and chopped*
2 *medium cloves garlic, peeled and minced*

2 *8-ounce cans tomato sauce*
½ *tablespoon salt*
⅛ *teaspoon black pepper*
1 *medium stalk celery, minced*

Wash and pick over the beans and place them in a large heavy kettle or a Dutch oven with the water and stir in the remaining ingredients. Bring to a boil, cover, and cook over medium heat for about 3 hours, or until the beans are very soft. After the first 1½ hours check occasionally to make sure water isn't boiling away. If it is, add more.

SERVES 12

Pickled Blackeye Beans

This is really a relish that goes well with cold or hot grilled meats.

2 cups cooked or canned
    blackeye beans, drained
½ cup cider vinegar
2 teaspoons granulated sugar
1 teaspoon salt
⅛ teaspoon black pepper

¼ cup diced sweet or dill pickles
3 tablespoons minced yellow
    onion
2 tablespoons minced sweet red
    pepper

Place the beans in a large bowl. Warm the vinegar and stir in the sugar. Add the salt and pepper to the vinegar and pour the mixture over the beans. Mix well, add the remaining ingredients, and combine well.

SERVES 6

Blackeyes with Chicken

The herbs here, combined, make up a fines herbes mixture: You can use dried mixed fines herbes instead of the fresh if the fresh aren't available. If you don't have chervil, double the amount of parsley.

1½ to 2 pounds chicken, cut up
½ cup all-purpose flour
3 tablespoons vegetable oil
3 tablespoons butter or
    margarine
4 tablespoons minced yellow
    onion
½ pound mushrooms, wiped
    clean and quartered
1 medium clove garlic, peeled
    and minced
1 teaspoon salt

⅛ teaspoon black pepper
¼ teaspoon minced parsley
¼ teaspoon minced chives
¼ teaspoon minced chervil
¼ teaspoon minced tarragon
½ cup dry white wine or
    chicken broth
4 cups cooked or canned
    blackeye beans, drained
1 medium tomato, chopped
About ½ cup chicken broth or
    bean liquid

1. Toss the chicken parts with the flour. Heat the oil and the butter or margarine in a large skillet and brown the chicken over medium heat on all sides, about 20 minutes. Remove the chicken with a slotted spoon and keep warm.

2. Add the onion and mushrooms to the skillet, then the garlic, salt, pepper, and herbs and sauté together 5 to 7 minutes. Add the wine or chicken broth, scrape up the pan juices, then add the blackeyes and heat to boiling. Push the chicken pieces down into the beans slightly. Sprinkle tomato over the top and add enough chicken broth or bean liquid so a little shows through the beans. Cover and simmer 20 minutes, or until chicken is tender.

SERVES 4 to 6

Shrimp Creole with Blackeyes

This blackeye dish includes rice (which makes it especially nutritious) and goes easy on the expensive shrimp. I buy frozen shrimp by the large bagful at the supermarket, measure out what I need, and freeze the rest. Six ounces of frozen shrimp is about 1¼ cups.

¼ cup butter or margarine	⅛ teaspoon black pepper
1 medium yellow onion, peeled and chopped	Dash of Tabasco sauce
1 large clove garlic, peeled and minced	2 cups cooked parboiled rice
	½ cup shredded medium-sharp Cheddar cheese
1 medium green pepper, seeded and chopped	2 cups cooked or canned blackeye beans
2 8-ounce cans tomato sauce	1 6-ounce package frozen shrimp, shelled and deveined
1 teaspoon salt	

1. Melt half the butter or margarine in a small saucepan. Add the onion, garlic, green pepper, tomato sauce, salt, pepper, and Tabasco sauce. Simmer, stirring occasionally, for about 10 minutes.

2. Heat the oven to 350°F.

3. Line the bottoms and sides of a 1½-quart casserole with the rice and sprinkle the cheese over it. Drain the beans, reserving the liquid. Fill the casserole with beans, add the shrimp, and spoon

½ cup of the onion mixture over them. Bake 10 or 20 minutes, or until the shrimp are cooked. If the dish dries, add reserved bean liquid. Heat the remaining sauce to bubbling, and sprinkle over the casserole just before serving.

SERVES 4 to 6

Blackeye Supper

This is a cheesy blackeye casserole that's easy on the budget, high in nutrition, and popular with most kids.

3 cups cooked or canned blackeyes, drained	2 tablespoons all-purpose flour
4 tablespoons butter or margarine, softened	¾ cup milk
	¾ cup grated medium-sharp Cheddar cheese
1 teaspoon curry powder	2 to 3 frankfurters
¼ teaspoon salt	

1. Heat the oven to 350°F.
2. Empty the beans into a 1½-quart casserole, and spread them into a smooth layer.
3. Melt 2 tablespoons butter or margarine in a small skillet over low heat and stir in the curry powder, salt, and flour to make a smooth paste. Add the milk and stir until sauce smooths and thickens. Mix in the Cheddar cheese and cook, stirring, until the cheese has melted.
4. Pour the cheese sauce over the beans. Split the frankfurters lengthwise and arrange over the bean mixture. Brush 2 tablespoons soft butter over the top and bake until lightly browned and bubbly.

SERVES 2 to 3

Blackeyes, Brazilian Style

This version of a typically Latin dish is from the West Coast. If Monterey Jack cheese isn't available in your area, substitute cream cheese or a mild Cheddar.

2⅔ cups (1 pound) dry
    blackeye beans
    Water to cover beans
¼ cup butter or margarine
¾ cup chopped yellow onion
1 large clove garlic, peeled
    and minced
1½ tablespoons all-purpose flour

1½ cups whole milk
2½ tablespoons prepared mustard
½ teaspoon salt
¼ teaspoon black pepper
½ pound Monterey Jack cheese,
    cut into cubes
1 pound pork sausages

1. Wash and pick over the beans. Cover with water, bring to a boil, and cook ¾ hour, or until tender. Drain.

2. Melt the butter or margarine in a large skillet and add the onion and garlic. Sauté about 5 minutes, or until the onion is translucent. Stir in the flour, and when you have a smooth paste, stir in the milk all at once. Keep stirring until the sauce is smooth, then add the mustard, salt, and pepper. Stir in the beans and ¾ of the cheese.

3. In a medium skillet over medium-high heat brown the sausages about 10 minutes and drain.

4. Heat the oven to 350°F.

5. Turn the bean mixture into a 2-quart casserole. Arrange the sausages over the top and sprinkle with the remaining cheese. Bake, uncovered, 30 minutes, or until the cheese has melted.

SERVES 8 to 10

Chicken à la Blackeye

This is a great way to use leftover chicken and blackeye beans. Nice on crisp toast points. If you don't have pimiento, a single cut-up canned tomato (drained) will add the necessary color. Chicken fat is rendered when a chicken is roasted. Pour it off and chill it—it's great for cooking. For a meatier dish add more chicken.

3 tablespoons chicken fat,
    butter, or margarine
3 tablespoons all-purpose flour
1½ cups whole milk
1 teaspoon salt
⅛ teaspoon black pepper

1 tablespoon dry sherry
1 cup cooked chicken, cubed
1½ cups cooked or canned
    blackeye beans, drained
¼ cup canned pimiento,
    drained and diced

Melt the chicken fat in a large saucepan over low heat and stir the flour into it to make a smooth paste. Add the milk all at once and stir quickly to make a smooth sauce; stir until sauce thickens. Add salt and pepper. When the sauce is thick, add sherry and the chicken, and, when it has heated, add the beans and pimiento and cook until hot.

SERVES 3 to 4

Blackeye Chili

A chili casserole that includes meat and makes an excellent dinner. This can be made in a slow cooker using twice as much water as dry beans. Just follow step 1, then scrape the meat mixture and remaining ingredients into the slow cooker and cook 8 to 10 hours, or until the beans are tender, on the low-heat setting; 4 to 6 cups of water may be enough.

3 tablespoons vegetable oil
2 pounds ground beef
2 cups chopped yellow onion
½ cup chopped celery
3 peeled cloves garlic, sliced
1 large green pepper, seeded
  and chopped
1 pound dry blackeyes

8 cups cold water
2 tablespoons salt
1 tablespoon granulated sugar
2 teaspoons chili powder
1 teaspoon Tabasco sauce
2 28-ounce cans whole tomatoes
  Salt and black pepper to taste

1. Heat the oil in a 6-quart kettle or a Dutch oven over medium heat and sauté the beef, onion, celery, garlic, and green pepper until the meat is well browned.
2. Add the beans, water, and remaining ingredients; cover, bring to a boil, boil 2 minutes, lower the heat to simmer, and simmer 4 hours, or until beans are tender. After the first 2 hours check the pot to make sure water isn't boiling away. Add more if needed. If the liquid is too thin at the end of cooking period, boil rapidly, stirring to prevent burning, until the mixture has thickened. Check seasoning and add pepper and more salt if needed before serving.

SERVES 8 to 10

Blackeye and Vegetable Skillet

Chili sauce or catsup can be used instead of the barbecue sauce in this recipe.

8 *slices bacon*	6 *cups cooked or canned*
2 *large yellow onions, peeled*	*blackeye beans, drained*
and chopped	2 *cups bean liquid*
2 *medium stalks celery, sliced*	½ *cup barbecue sauce*
¼ *inch thick*	1 *teaspoon prepared mustard*
2 *small carrots, scraped and*	1 *cup seeded, diced green pepper*
sliced ¼ inch thick	

1. Cook the bacon in a large skillet over medium heat until all the fat is rendered and bacon is crisp. Remove the bacon.

2. Add the onions, celery, and carrots to the bacon fat; sauté, stirring, until the onion is translucent.

3. Add the beans, bean liquid, barbecue sauce, and mustard to the skillet, mix well, and simmer 15 minutes more. About 3 minutes before the end mix in the pepper and stir until it has softened a little. Serve mixture topped with crumbled bacon.

SERVES 8

Blackeye Bean Casserole

Butter or margarine	3 *tablespoons grated yellow*
8 *frankfurters, halved and sliced*	*onion*
into ⅛-inch-wide pieces	¾ *teaspoon dry mustard*
4 *cups cooked or canned*	¼ *teaspoon powdered or ground*
blackeyes, drained	*thyme*
¼ *pound fresh mushrooms,*	¼ *teaspoon black pepper*
wiped clean and sliced	1 *cup grated medium-sharp*
1 *15-ounce can tomato sauce*	*Cheddar cheese*

1. Heat the oven to 350°F.

2. Melt 1 tablespoon butter or margarine in a large skillet over medium heat and sauté the frankfurters until medium brown. In

a large casserole combine the frankfurters, beans, mushrooms, and remaining ingredients except the cheese. Bake for 25 minutes, then sprinkle the cheese on top, dot with more butter, and broil at medium heat until the cheese melts and begins to brown.

SERVES 6 to 8

Blackeye Hash

3½ cups cooked or canned
    blackeyes
3 tablespoons bacon drippings
1 medium yellow onion, minced
½ 15-ounce can corned beef
    hash

1 tablespoon soy sauce
1 teaspoon salt
⅛ teaspoon black pepper
Catsup

1. Drain the beans and reserve the liquid.
2. Melt the bacon drippings in a large skillet over medium heat and sauté the onion in it until it is translucent. Add the hash, beans, and ½ cup bean liquid and mix thoroughly. Add soy sauce, salt, and pepper. Taste and add more seasonings if desired. Cover, lower the heat, and cook about 10 minutes. Add more bean liquid if the dish dries out. Serve with catsup.

SERVES 4 to 6

13

Garbanzo Beans (Chick-Peas)

Like yellow-eye or blackeye beans, garbanzos, which are also called chick-peas, *aren't* members of the common bean family. But unlike blackeyes and yellow eyes, they don't look like common shell beans. They're attractive, creamy-yellow-colored legumes that look a bit like large filberts. They're especially popular in Portugal and Spain; and chances are you've had them in Italian antipasto plates (one such recipe, Garbanzo Antipasto—pages 150–151—follows), done up in a vinaigrette sauce and sitting near the anchovies. The flavor of garbanzos is nutlike, the texture when dry and cooked is mealy, and they mix very well indeed with other beans, particularly the reds. They're especially good in salads and appetizers.

The Garbanzo Cocktail Dip (page 150) is a takeoff on a Middle Eastern dish called Hummus and is tasty served with Arabic or Indian bread rounds. Garbanzo Soup, Spanish Style (pages 151–152), includes ham hocks and pepperoni and is a popular Latin recipe, as is the Chicken Casserole Enchilada (page 159), a quick version of a Mexican recipe. A Latin dish, Garbanzo Chili Pot (pages 156–157), has been included along with the basically Italian Garbanzo Casserole with Biscuit Topping (pages 157–158). Garbanzos, East Indian Style (page 156), is a good introduction to Far Eastern cooking.

Garbanzos go particularly well with chicken, as in Garbanzo Chicken Casserole (page 158), and should inspire you to incorporate garbanzos in your own favorite chicken stew recipe.

The largest group of garbanzo bean recipes here, however, is the salads. Garbanzos go well with fruits such as peaches and make good salad combinations with any of the other beans.

Garbanzo Cocktail Dip

This resembles a Middle East dip called Hummus. If your supermarket sells Arabic or Indian bread, cut into wedges, and offer with the dip.

*2 cups cooked or canned
   garbanzos, drained; reserve
   ¼ cup liquid and a few
   whole garbanzos
2 tablespoons sesame oil or
   olive oil*
3 tablespoons strained lemon juice*

*1 large clove garlic, peeled
¼ teaspoon ground cumin
¼ cup garbanzo liquid or ¼
   cup beef bouillon
1 teaspoon salt
¼ teaspoon black pepper*

1. Place all the ingredients, except the reserved garbanzos and liquid, in the blender, turn it on to a low speed, and add the ¼ cup garbanzo liquid or beef bouillon a little at a time until the mixture has been reduced to the consistency of very thick batter.

2. Taste and add more lemon juice, garlic, salt, and pepper if desired. Turn into serving bowl. Garnish with the reserved garbanzos.

YIELDS 1½ cups

* If you use olive oil instead of sesame oil, increase the quantity of sesame seeds to ¼ cup.

Antipasto Garbanzo

Italian restaurants serve garbanzos this way in a plate of mixed antipasto, but the dish also makes a fine luncheon salad. It is best when garbanzos are freshly cooked and combined with ingredients while still warm.

*1 cup cooked or canned
    garbanzos, drained
1 8-ounce package bologna,
    finely diced
½ cup finely chopped celery
½ cup finely chopped yellow
    onion
½ cup finely chopped green
    pepper
1 4-ounce jar pimiento, drained
    and chopped*

*3 stalks cooked broccoli
3 tablespoons red wine vinegar
¼ cup vegetable oil
    Salt and freshly ground black
        pepper to taste
¼ teaspoon chili powder
1 medium clove garlic, peeled
    and minced
3 tablespoons finely minced
    fresh parsley*

In a large bowl combine garbanzos and all remaining ingredients except parsley. Toss well, cover, and chill. Before serving, toss again and garnish with parsley.

SERVES 10 to 12

Garbanzo Soup, Spanish Style

Pepperonis are those hot little Italian sausages, and they give this soup-cum-main dish a very spicy flavor. This dish is nice with crusty Italian bread. Step 1 can be done in a slow cooker: Cook on the low-heat setting for 6 to 8 hours, or until ham hock meat is tender enough to fall off the bone. If there's too much liquid at the end of the cooking period, boil it down to your taste; it should be thick.

*2 cups dry garbanzos
2 quarts water
2 fresh ham hocks
1 large bay leaf
½ cup vegetable oil
2 large yellow onions, peeled
    and minced
2 large cloves garlic, peeled
    and minced*

*½ cup diced green pepper
10 to 16 ounce pepperoni, diced
3 large potatoes, peeled and
    diced
1 medium carrot, peeled and
    diced
    Salt and black pepper to taste
1 teaspoon finely minced parsley*

1. Combine beans with water, ham hocks, and bay leaf in a large kettle and simmer 3 hours, or until meat is very tender.

2. Remove the meat from the bones, discard the bones, chop the meat, and return to the kettle.

3. Heat the oil in a large skillet over medium heat and simmer the onions, garlic, and green pepper in the oil until onions are translucent, about 5 minutes. Scrape mixture into the kettle with remaining ingredients, except the parsley, and simmer, uncovered, until potatoes are very tender. Garnish with parsley before serving.

SERVES 8 to 10

Beef Dinner Soup

If you have beef roast drippings or bacon fat to use, they will improve the flavor of this dish. Converted rice, the late Adele Davis said, is the most nutritious of the refined white rices. I find it the easiest kind to cook with; but other types of rice can be used. (Brown rice will need to cook longer than white rice.) Two pounds of stew beef and a lot of vegetables make this thick, tempting fragrant stew a fine one-dish dinner. Serve with Indian bread or dinner rolls and butter and a tossed green salad.

2 *pounds stew beef, cut into*
   ½-inch pieces
3 *tablespoons all-purpose flour*
2 *tablespoons curry powder*
2 *teaspoons salt*
¼ *teaspoon black pepper*
3 *tablespoons beef roast*
   drippings or shortening
1 *large yellow onion, peeled and*
   coarsely chopped

4 *cups hot water, combined with*
   4 beef bouillon cubes
1 *16-ounce can whole tomatoes*
2 *cups cooked or canned*
   garbanzos, drained
3 *medium carrots, peeled and*
   diced
½ *cup raw converted rice*
1 *10-ounce package frozen peas*
½ *medium cucumber, peeled*

1. Dredge the beef in the flour combined with the curry powder, salt, and pepper. Melt the drippings or shortening in a large Dutch oven, or a kettle over medium-high heat and brown the beef well all over. When half done, add the onion; stir until onion is limp,

about 5 minutes. Add the beef bouillon, lower the heat, scrape up the browned bits, cover, and simmer 1 hour.

2. Stir again and add the tomatoes, beans, carrots, and rice; cover and simmer another 30 minutes. Add the peas; then the cucumbers cut in half and sliced across. Stir and simmer 15 minutes more.

SERVES 8

Onion and Garbanzo Salad

If you like onions, this is your dish. It can be made with ordinary yellow onions, but it is meant to be made with those big, sweet onions called Spanish or Bermuda onions. Italian parsley is less finely curled than French, and has a slightly stronger flavor.

1 *large sweet onion, peeled and sliced thin*
Iced water to cover onion
¼ *cup olive or vegetable oil*
2 *tablespoons red wine vinegar*
1 *teaspoon salt*
½ *teaspoon dried (or 1 teaspoon fresh) oregano*
⅛ *teaspoon red pepper*
1 *cup cooked or canned garbanzos, drained*

1 *large tomato, stem end removed, cut into wedges*
1 *green pepper, seeded and sliced into thin rings*
6 *pitted green olives, sliced into rings*
6 *pitted ripe black olives, sliced into rings*
1 *small bunch Italian parsley, coarsely chopped*
1 *head romaine lettuce*

1. Separate the onion into rings and cover with iced water. Add a few ice cubes. Soak 30 minutes, then drain and pat dry with paper towels. In a large bowl combine the oil, vinegar, and seasonings. Toss the onion in the dressing, cover, and chill several hours.

2. Combine onion with the beans, tomato, green pepper, and green and black olives and scoop into a salad bowl lined with romaine lettuce. Garnish with parsley.

SERVES 6

Peaches and Garbanzo Salad

This combination of peaches and garbanzos is slightly sweet, a good side dish with bland meats like ham and pork.

1 29-ounce can cling peaches
2 cups cooked or canned
   garbanzos, drained
½ green pepper, seeded, minced
1 cup celery, diced
2 cups shredded lettuce
3 tablespoons vegetable oil

*3 tablespoons tarragon vinegar**
1 tablespoon minced parsley
¼ teaspoon dried tarragon (or
   ½ teaspoon fresh, minced)
¼ teaspoon curry powder
¼ teaspoon prepared mustard
1 small slice yellow onion

   1. Drain the peaches (reserving the syrup) and slice; place in a large salad bowl. Rinse the beans in cold water, drain, and combine with peaches, pepper, celery, and lettuce.

   2. Place 3 tablespoons reserved syrup and the remaining ingredients in the blender, or in a small jar, covered. Blend until smooth. Pour over the salad and combine well. Chill, if desired, before serving.

SERVES 6

* If you don't have tarragon vinegar, simmer 3 tablespoons plus ½ teaspoon plain white wine vinegar for a few minutes with 1 teaspoon dried tarragon, strain, and use that instead.

California Sunshine Salad

A beautiful salad mixture that is great with the Golden Gate Salad Dressing (page 155) or with Quick Mayonnaise Chantilly (page 172).

2 cups cooked or canned
   garbanzos, drained
1 8¾-ounce can whole kernel
   corn
1 cup diced celery
½ cup minced yellow onion

¼ cup diced green pepper
3 tablespoons diced canned
   pimiento
1¾ cups Golden Gate Salad
   Dressing (page 155)

Combine all the ingredients except dressing in a large, clear salad bowl, moisten to taste with dressing, cover, and chill slightly. Serve with remaining dressing on the side.

SERVES 6 to 8

Golden Gate Salad Dressing

For use with California Sunshine Salad (pages 154–155) or Jellied Bean Salad (pages 171).

⅓ *cup granulated sugar*	½ *cup vinegar*
1 *teaspoon salt*	½ *cup water*
½ *teaspoon dry mustard*	1 *tablespoons butter or*
2 *tablespoons all-purpose flour*	*margarine*
2 *egg yolks*	

1. Mix the dry ingredients in a small bowl. In a medium bowl with a narrow bottom beat the egg yolks with a fork and then beat in the dry mixture.

2. Heat the remaining ingredients to boiling in a small saucepan, then at once begin to sprinkle the hot mixture into the egg yolks, stirring very rapidly. Turn the mixture back into the saucepan, and over very low heat cook, stirring constantly. Don't let the mixture boil. In 2 or 3 minutes the sauce should be thick and smooth. Remove from the heat and chill before serving.

YIELDS 1¾ cups

Garbanzos, East Indian Style

Flavored with mint and ginger, this is a good side dish for an Oriental meal or grilled meats.

¼ *cup butter or margarine*
2 *medium yellow onions,*
    peeled and finely chopped
2 *teaspoons salt*
1½ *teaspoons ground turmeric*
    or curry powder
½ *teaspoon ground ginger*

¼ *teaspoon ground dried mint*
2 *medium, fresh or canned*
    tomatoes, peeled and
    chopped
2 *cups cooked or canned*
    garbanzos, drained
1½ *cups beef bouillon*

Melt the butter or margarine in a large skillet over medium heat, add the onions, and cook until the onions are translucent, 5 to 10 minutes. Add all remaining ingredients except the garbanzos and bouillon and simmer, stirring, 10 minutes. Add the garbanzos and bouillon, cover, and simmer 20 minutes more. Check in 10 minutes to make sure there is still a good amount of bouillon; add more if needed. Serve hot.

SERVES 4

Garbanzo Chili Pot

This is a soup that serves as the main course. It's nice with fresh corn bread and butter with a green salad tossed with French dressing. If you have a slow cooker, brown the meat, scrape pan juices as directed into the cooker, and cook on the low-heat setting with remaining ingredients overnight, 10 to 12 hours, or until meat is very tender. Remove bones before serving. If there's too much liquid left, boil it down in an open kettle until the consistency is just right. Check seasonings before serving.

1 cup dry garbanzo beans,
    washed and soaked
    according to package
    directions
1 teaspoon vegetable oil
2½ pounds beef short ribs
1 28-ounce can whole tomatoes
2 medium yellow onions,
    peeled and chopped
1 cup minced celery
2 cloves garlic, peeled and
    minced
1 tablespoon salt
1¾ teaspoons chili powder
½ teaspoon ground black
    pepper
1 medium bay leaf
1½ teaspoons ground cumin

1. Drain the soaked beans and reserve the liquid.

2. Heat the oil in a large Dutch oven or a heavy kettle over medium-high heat and brown the ribs on all sides thoroughly. Add 1 quart bean soaking liquid, scrape up the pan juices, and add the drained beans. Cover and simmer 2 hours.

3. Remove the ribs and discard the bones. Mince the meat and return to the soup. Add the remaining ingredients and simmer 1 hour longer. If liquid evaporates, add more bean soaking water.

SERVES 8

Garbanzo Casserole with Biscuit Topping

A hearty dish with a biscuit topping and an Italian flavor. Nice with crisp, tossed green salad in Italian dressing. To make this ahead of time, cook the meat sauce overnight on low-heat setting in a slow cooker, combine with the garbanzos, and top with biscuits just before baking.

1 large yellow onion, peeled
    and minced
2 large cloves garlic, peeled
    and minced
3 tablespoons vegetable oil
1½ pounds ground meat
1 16-ounce can whole tomatoes
1 6-ounce can tomato paste
2½ cups water
1 teaspoon granulated sugar
2 teaspoons salt
¼ teaspoon black pepper
1 teaspoon dried basil
1 tablespoon dried oregano
2 large green peppers, seeded
    and chopped
2 cups cooked or canned
    garbanzos, drained
2 cups packaged biscuit mix

1. Sauté the onion and garlic in the oil in a large, heavy kettle or skillet over medium heat until onion is a little brown. Add the meat and cook, stirring, until meat is well browned. (Some of the onion may be very dark by then.) Stir in tomatoes, tomato paste, water, and remaining ingredients except garbanzos and biscuit mix. Simmer until the sauce is thick, stirring occasionally—about 45 minutes or 1 hour. If necessary, add more water. Add garbanzos, cover, and simmer while preparing biscuit mix according to package directions (do not bake).

2. Heat the oven to 425°F.

3. Turn the meat and bean mixture into a 12- by 8-inch baking dish and top with large spoonfuls of biscuit dough. Bake 25 to 30 minutes, or until the biscuits are done.

SERVES 8

Garbanzo Chicken Casserole

An unusual combination that should inspire you to devise some chicken and garbanzo bean dishes of your own. Wipe mushrooms clean with damp paper towels before chopping, unless they are really dirty; in that case, wash them and wipe them dry.

6 medium half-chicken breasts,
    or other chicken parts
½ cup all-purpose flour
½ teaspoon salt
⅛ teaspoon black pepper
2 tablespoons vegetable oil
3 tablespoons butter or
    margarine
4 tablespoons chopped yellow
    onion
½ pound mushrooms, wiped
    and chopped

¼ cup minced fresh parsley
½ cup dry white wine, or ½ cup
    chicken bouillon combined
    with 2 tablespoons strained
    lemon juice
3 cups cooked or canned
    garbanzos, drained
⅛ teaspoon curry powder
1 medium, fresh or canned
    tomato, diced

1. Toss the chicken in the flour, salt, and pepper, either in a paper bag or in a large bowl. Heat the oil and butter or margarine in a large skillet over medium heat and brown the chicken well on all sides.

2. Remove the chicken to a bowl and keep it warm. Add more

butter to the skillet if needed, and over medium heat brown the onion and mushrooms until the onion is translucent. Add remaining ingredients except tomato and scrape up pan juices. Place the chicken on top of the beans, garnish with tomato, cover, and cook 30 more minutes over medium-low heat. If contents dry, add a little more wine or chicken broth.

SERVES 6

Chicken Casserole Enchilada

A quick way to make a Mexican-flavored main course. Most supermarkets carry enchilada sauce and green chilis. Chicken back and giblets from the cut-up fryer can be saved to make soup. Remove the chicken wings and save them in the freezer; when you have a dozen or a dozen and a half, remove the wing tips and use the wings to make the casserole.

1 medium fryer, cut up	*1 10¾-ounce can condensed*
½ cup flour	*cream of chicken soup*
1 teaspoon salt	*⅔ cup evaporated milk*
¼ teaspoon black pepper	*1 tablespoon chopped, canned*
2 tablespoons vegetable oil	*green chilis*
1 medium yellow onion, peeled	*2 cups cooked or canned*
and chopped	*garbanzos, drained*
1 10-ounce can mild enchilada	*2 tablespoons minced parsley*
sauce	

1. Heat the oven to 350°F.
2. Dredge the chicken in the flour combined with salt and pepper and brown the chicken pieces in the oil in a large skillet over medium heat. Brown chicken well. Add the onion to the skillet and cook until translucent, 5 to 10 minutes.
3. Combine the enchilada sauce, soup, milk, and chilis and pour into the skillet. Quickly scrape up the pan juices then turn the contents of the skillet into a 3-quart casserole. Cover and bake 45 minutes.
4. Add beans, mix well, cover, and bake another 15 minutes. Garnish with parsley before serving.

SERVES 4 to 6

14

Black Beans

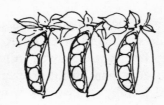

Black beans have a delightful, strong, nutty flavor all their own and a color that shows up wonderfully in salads. It should, for they really are black! Their cooking juices are equally dark. That's why Black Bean Soup (pages 160–161), for instance, *must* be made with black beans: There are no other beans that can act as a stand-in in this recipe.

Black Bean Soup ✓

Black bean soup is the best-known black bean recipe. Here's one version.

2 *cups dry black beans*	½ *cup minced yellow onion*
2 *quarts cold water*	2 *teaspoons salt*
2 *stalks celery, minced*	1½ *tablespoons all-purpose flour*
¼ *teaspoon black pepper*	1 *tablespoon cider vinegar*
¼ *teaspoon dry mustard*	10 *thin slices lemon*
⅛ *teaspoon dried thyme*	2 *shelled hardboiled eggs,*
2 *tablespoons butter or*	*sliced*
margarine	

1. Wash and pick over the beans. Combine with the water in a large saucepan. Bring to a boil, let boil 2 minutes, remove from the heat, cover, and let stand 1 hour. Add celery, pepper, mustard, and thyme.

2. Melt 1 tablespoon butter or margarine in a small saucepan and sauté the onion until translucent. Add to the beans, cover, and simmer the beans until very tender, 2 to 3 hours.

3. Add the salt. A little at a time blend the beans smooth in the blender or press them through a food mill. There should be about 7 cups.

4. Melt the remaining tablespoon of butter in a small saucepan and stir in the flour to make a smooth paste. Add ½ cup of the hot bean soup and stir quickly to make a smooth sauce. Scrape sauce back into the soup and simmer about 3 minutes. Add the vinegar. Taste and add more salt if needed. Float a slice of lemon and a slice of hardboiled egg in each serving.

SERVES 10

Coach House Black Bean Soup

This is from Elaine Light's wonderful cookbook, *Gourmets and Groundhogs*.* It is a little more elaborate than the preceding recipe, but it makes use of a leftover hambone and the rind from the hambone. Using leftovers always makes me happy!

4 cups dried black beans	4 bay leaves
5 quarts cold water	1 tablespoon salt
3 stalks celery, chopped	½ teaspoon freshly ground black
3 large onions, chopped	pepper
½ cup butter	1 cup dry Madeira
2½ tablespoons flour	2 hard cooked eggs, finely
½ cup parsley, chopped	chopped
Hambone and rind	Thin lemon slices
3 leeks, thinly sliced	

1. Pick over and wash beans. Soak overnight in cold water to cover. Drain, add 5 quarts of cold water, and simmer over low heat 1½ hours.

2. In a soup kettle, sauté slowly celery and onions in butter until tender, about 8 minutes. Blend in flour and parsley and cook, stirring, for 1 minute. Gradually stir in beans and their liquid. Add hambone and rind, leeks, bay leaves, salt and pepper.

3. Simmer soup over very low heat for 4 hours. Remove and discard hambone, rind, and bay leaves and force the beans through a sieve (do not use a blender). Combine the strained beans with their broth and Madeira. Bring soup to a boil, remove it from the heat, and stir in eggs. Float a thin slice of lemon on each serving.

SERVES 8 to 10

* Elaine Light, *Gourmets and Groundhogs.* (Dubois, Pa.: Gray Printing Company), 1968. Reprinted with the author's permission.

Baked Black Beans ✓

A simple savory dish that is delicious with any grilled meat.

1⅓ cups dry black beans
    Cold water to cover beans
1 large yellow onion, peeled
    and chopped
3 cloves garlic, peeled and
    minced
2 carrots, peeled and grated
2 celery stalks, chopped
1 red (or green), pepper,
    seeded and chopped
2 tablespoons vegetable oil

1 medium bay leaf
4 tablespoons finely minced
    fresh parsley
½ teaspoon dried thyme
4 tablespoons light rum
    (optional)
6 whole black peppercorns
4 tablespoons butter or
    margarine
2 teaspoons salt (or to taste)

1. Wash and pick over the beans. Cover with cold water and bring to a boil in a large Dutch oven. Boil 2 minutes, remove from the heat, cover, and let stand about 1 hour.

2. Heat oven to 350°F.

3. In a large skillet sauté the onion, garlic, and vegetables in the oil over medium heat until onions are translucent. Combine vegetables with beans and soaking liquid. Add bay leaf, parsley, thyme, rum, and peppercorns. Cover, bring to a boil, lower heat, and bake at 350°F. for 2 hours or until completely tender. Check occasionally to make sure water hasn't run out.

4. Just a few minutes before beans are ready to serve, add butter or margarine and salt. Before serving, taste and add more salt if needed.

SERVES 4 to 6

Black Beans and Rice

Beautifully white buttered rice ringed with black beans makes a really handsome side dish for any roast and tastes especially nice with pork or ham.

1⅓ cups dry black beans
    Cold water to cover beans
1 small yellow onion, peeled
1 small bay leaf
¼ teaspoon dry thyme
    Salt to taste
3 tablespoons butter or
    margarine

1½ cups converted rice
3 cups cold water
1 tablespoon butter or
    margarine
1½ teaspoons salt
2 tablespoons finely minced
    fresh parsley
    Dash of paprika

1. Wash and pick over beans. Cover with cold water and bring to a boil. Boil 2 minutes, remove from the heat, cover, and let stand about 1 hour.

2. Return to the heat, add the onion, cover, bring to a boil, add bay leaf and thyme, reduce heat, and simmer 2 or 3 hours, covered, or until beans are tender but not breaking. Check during this period to make sure beans aren't drying out, and add a little water if needed. When beans are done, remove onion and bay, add salt to taste, and toss gently with butter or margarine.

3. Half an hour before beans are ready, place rice in a large saucepan with water, butter or margarine, and salt; cover and bring to a boil, then reduce heat and simmer 10 to 12 minutes or until all water has been absorbed and rice is tender. Keep covered until ready to serve.

4. Heap rice in center of a large platter, and spoon beans around the rice; sprinkle a few beans over the rice just to show the contrast in color. Sprinkle minced parsley and paprika over the rice.

SERVES 6 to 8

Black Beans and Black Pudding

This is another Spanish specialty. Black pudding, *morcilla*, is a variation of the sausage called blood pudding in Scotland and Canada—a highly seasoned sausage made with blood. The Spanish make this with *alubias* (red beans).

1⅓ cups dry black beans
    Cold water to cover beans
1 *large yellow onion, peeled*
    and chopped
¾ *pound thick bacon, cut into*
    1-inch pieces

½ *pound potatoes, peeled and*
    cut into thick slices
¼ *pound chorizo or hot Italian*
    sausage
¼ *pound blood pudding*
    Salt to taste

1. Wash and pick over the beans. Cover with cold water in a Dutch oven. Bring to a boil, boil 2 minutes, remove from the heat, cover, and let stand 1 hour.

2. Return to the heat and add the onion and bacon. Cover and bring to a boil, then reduce the heat and simmer 30 minutes. Add the potatoes, then add the chorizo and blood pudding, pricked all over with a fork. Cover and simmer until the potatoes and beans are tender, 2 to 2½ hours. Add a little cold water if the beans are drying out.

3. Remove the sausages from the beans, slice, and strew over the beans before serving. Taste the beans and add salt if needed.

SERVES 4 to 6

Black Beans, Spanish Style

In Spain this dish is made with the red bean called *alubia*. Black beans are considered the best substitute here.

2⅔ cups dry black beans
    Water to cover beans
¼ *pound thick sliced bacon in*
    1-inch strips
1 *large yellow onion, peeled*
    and sliced

1 *tablespoon olive oil*
¼ *pound chorizo or hot Italian*
    sausage
    Salt and pepper to taste

1. Wash and pick over the beans. Combine with water to cover in a large saucepan, bring to a boil, boil 2 minutes, remove from the heat, cover, and let stand 1 hour.

2. Return to the heat and add the bacon and half the onion. Cover, bring to a boil, reduce the heat, and simmer 1 hour.

3. Heat the oil in a small skillet and sauté the remaining onion until it is translucent, about 5 minutes, then scrape into the beans, with the chorizo or Italian sausage left whole but pricked all over with a fork. Add a little cold water if the beans are drying out. Cover and cook until the beans are tender but not mushy, about 1½ hours. Add salt and pepper.

3. Remove the sausage from the beans, slice, and strew over the beans before serving.

SERVES 6

Lobster with Black Beans, Canton

Big chunks of lobster in a typically Cantonese sauce. South African frozen rock lobster tails are a good substitute for fresh lobster tails and in my area less expensive. Use two 9-ounce packages. Serve with rice. From *Oriental Cooking the Fast Wok Way.*

¼ cup oil
2 teaspoons preserved Chinese black beans, or soy sauce
2 cloves garlic, peeled, minced
¼ pound (½ cup) lean ground pork
1 tablespoon soy sauce
1 teaspoon salt
⅛ teaspoon ground ginger
½ teaspoon sugar
¼ teaspoon black pepper
1 scallion, minced, or 1 tablespoon minced onion
1 pound lobster tails, shelled
1 cup chicken stock, or water
2 tablespoons cornstarch
3 tablespoons water
2 eggs, slightly beaten

1. Measure and prepare ingredients as listed; cut lobster tails into 1-inch-thick slices across the grain. Mix cornstarch with water. Set ingredients by the stove in order listed and have handy a small bowl and a slotted spoon. Heat serving dish in 250° oven.

2. Set *wok* over high heat for 30 seconds, swirl in oil, count to 30, turn heat to medium. Add black beans and garlic, stir-fry until garlic begins to brown. Add pork and stir-fry 1 minute, remove to bowl with slotted spoon. Stir in soy sauce, salt, ginger, sugar, pepper, and scallion. Mix, then add lobster pieces and stir-fry 1 minute. Return pork to *wok*; mix. Swirl Chicken Stock and cornstarch mixture down side of *wok* and stir with juices until sauce begins to thicken and clear. Push solids to one side, dribble eggs into simmering sauce, stir and toss together all ingredients. Keep warm until ready to serve.

SERVES 2 to 4, more as part of a large meal

Steamed Sea Bass

This is a classic Chinese way of doing fish such as sea bass. From *Oriental Cooking the Fast Wok Way.*

2 tablespoons preserved black beans	1½ pounds fresh sea bass, head and tail included
1 tablespoon soy sauce	18 shreds fresh ginger root
1 tablespoon dry sherry	1 scallion in shreds 2 inches long
1 tablespoon oil	
½ teaspoon sugar	

1. Chop black beans and mix in a small bowl with soy sauce, sherry, oil, and sugar. Wash and dry cleaned fish. Make ½-inch-deep slashes every half inch down the meatiest part of each side of fish, from gills to tail. Make slashes deepest where fish is thickest. Set fish on its side on an ovenproof serving dish that will fit steaming equipment. Arrange black bean mixture attractively down the side of the fish so that juices run into gashes, and beans cover them. Place ginger shreds over beans in a pattern of x's that touch at top and base. Divide scallion shreds into 4 or 5 bunches, each including some green, and arrange bunches decoratively over ginger pattern. Place dish inside steamer.

2. Fill steamer base with boiling water to within an inch of

serving dish, bring water back to a rapid boil, cover, and steam fish 30 minutes, or until fish eye is white and protrudes. Add more water if necessary.

SERVES 3 to 4, more if other dishes are offered

15

Bean Combinations

I have always been enamored of multibean combinations. Their many flavors are intriguing, and they're quite attractive as well.

From Saint Croix in the Virgin Islands I have included here a remarkable salad that I call Black Beans and More Beans (page 175) that combines black beans with blackeyes, red kidney beans, baby limas, bean sprouts, green beans, and yellow wax beans. Much simpler is a popular version of Four Bean Salad (page 169), which contains red kidney beans, large whites, garbanzos, and blackeyes. The addition of a few leftover black beans would enhance this dish, too.

Fresh and Dry Bean Salad (pages 170–171) also contains four types of beans: Italian or plain green snap beans, yellow snap beans, blackeyes, and garbanzos. And Hawaiian Dinner Soup (page 180) includes up to seven kinds of beans: small whites, pintos, reds, kidneys, blackeyes, garbanzos, and limas.

Antipasto Supper (page 176) has only two kinds of beans—red kidney beans and garbanzos—but it's a particularly good combination and one of my favorite summertime recipes.

Four Bean Salad

This is one of the best-known mixed bean salads. It can be made with other bean combinations than those suggested here. Lima beans, big or small, are often included. The dressing proposed here is lemon flavored and tart; you may use 1 to 1½ cups of your favorite dressing and omit the oil, vinegar, lemon juice, salt, and pepper.

2 cups each cooked or canned
    dark or light red kidney
    beans, Great Northern
    beans, garbanzos, and
    blackeye beans; drained
1 very large Spanish onion,
    peeled and minced
½ cup washed, sliced radishes
1 large cucumber, peeled and
    diced

¼ cup chopped parsley
⅔ cup vegetable oil
¼ cup white vinegar
¼ cup strained lemon juice
1 teaspoon salt
¼ teaspoon black pepper
    Iceberg lettuce, washed and
    drained

1. Combine beans gently in a very large bowl with onion, radishes, cucumber, and parsley. In a small bowl beat together remaining ingredients except lettuce, then mix with beans. Cover and chill for at least 2 hours.
2. Line a large salad bowl with lettuce leaves and turn bean mixture into the bowl.

SERVES 8

Lima Bean and Garbanzo Salad

This is great picnic fare—tasty with broiled burgers, hot dogs, cold ham, etc.

1½ cups cooked or canned
    garbanzos, drained
1½ cups cooked or canned large
    lima beans, drained

½ cup chopped yellow onion
1 can pimientos, drained and
    diced
¾ cup Italian salad dressing

In a large bowl combine the beans with the remaining ingredients. Toss thoroughly, cover, and chill overnight.

SERVES 4 to 6

Italian Dressing

½ cup olive oil or vegetable oil
¼ cup red wine vinegar
⅛ teaspoon dry mustard
½ teaspoon granulated sugar
1 teaspoon salt

¼ teaspoon black pepper
1 teaspoon Italian salad dressing, herb blend
¼ teaspoon paprika

Combine all ingredients in the blender and blend on high speed for 30 seconds.

YIELDS ¾ cup

Fresh and Dry Bean Salad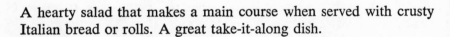

A hearty salad that makes a main course when served with crusty Italian bread or rolls. A great take-it-along dish.

1 teaspoon salt
1 small clove garlic, peeled
½ cup vegetable oil
½ cup white wine vinegar
2 tablespoons firmly packed light brown sugar
½ teaspoon prepared mustard, dried
½ teaspoon dried basil or 1 teaspoon fresh basil, minced
½ teaspoon dried tarragon or 1 teaspoon fresh tarragon, minced

2 packages frozen Italian-style green beans, cooked and drained
1 pound cooked or canned yellow snap beans, drained
2 cups cooked or canned blackeye beans, drained
2 cups cooked or canned garbanzos, drained
3 tablespoons minced fresh parsley
1 small Spanish onion, peeled and sliced into thin rings

1. In a large wooden bowl, sprinkle the salt, slice in the garlic, and thoroughly mash the garlic into the salt. Add the oil, wine vinegar, brown sugar, prepared mustard, basil, and tarragon and beat with a fork. Toss the beans in the dressing and chill.

2. Before serving, toss well once more, then sprinkle with parsley and garnish with onion rings.

SERVES 12

Jellied Bean Salad

This molded gelatin salad makes a colorful side dish that's great for bring-a-dish parties. The gelatin takes several hours to set, so make this the day before if you can.

⅔ cup each *of cooked or canned garbanzos; light-red kidney beans; and blackeye beans, drained*

¼ cup *drained and diced bread-and-butter pickles (reserve liquid)*

3 tablespoons *diced canned pimiento*

1 *6-ounce package lemon gelatin*

2½ cups *boiling water*

1 *head escarole, washed and drained (optional)*

1 *can mandarin oranges, drained (optional)*

1½ cups *Quick Mayonnaise Chantilly (page 172) or Golden Gate Salad Dressing (page 155)*

1. Combine beans with pickles and pimientos in a large mixing bowl.

2. Place the gelatin in another large bowl, stir in the boiling water until the gelatin is dissolved and add ¼ cup of the pickle liquid. Stir, then set in the freezer a few minutes until the liquid is cool. Over cracked ice stir until the gelatin becomes thick enough to hold up the beans. Stir bean mixture into the gelatin, turn into a 2-quart mold rinsed in cold water, and refrigerate until set.

3. Unmold onto a bed of escarole and garnish with mandarin oranges and Quick Mayonnaise Chantilly or Golden Gate Salad Dressing.

SERVES 6 to 8

Quick Mayonnaise Chantilly

For use in Jellied Bean Salad (page 171) or California Sunshine Salad (pages 154–155).

1 cup mayonnaise	*¼ teaspoon prepared mustard*
1 teaspoon strained lemon juice	*½ cup whipped cream*

Combine all ingredients, cover, and chill for a few hours before serving.

YIELDS 1½ cups

Red, Green, and Yellow Bean Salad

This is a delicious salad and so quick to make it's a delight. For best flavor, pour the dressing over the beans while they are slightly warm and let stand for a few hours at room temperature; then put in the refrigerator overnight. However, the salad also tastes just great made at the last minute and served at once. You can sliver the pepper by using a potato peeler.

½ seeded green pepper, slivered	*¼ cup red wine vinegar*
2 cups cooked or canned cut green beans, drained	*2 teaspoons salt*
2 cups cooked or canned cut yellow beans, drained	*¼ teaspoon dry mustard*
2 cups cooked or canned light red kidney beans, drained	*½ teaspoon granulated sugar*
1 cup vegetable oil	*¼ teaspoon black pepper*
	1 medium Spanish onion, peeled
	2 tablespoons minced parsley

In a large salad bowl combine the green pepper and beans. With the blender at a medium speed combine the remaining ingredients except onion and parsley; pour over the beans and pepper, and mix well. Use a potato peeler or a very sharp knife to sliver the onion over the beans and sprinkle with parsley. Toss again before serving.

SERVES 6 to 8

Beans in Sweet-and-Sour Dressing

This dish is best when all beans have been freshly cooked and drained and are combined with pickles and pimientos and dressing while the beans are still warm. Allow to cool, then cover and refrigerate.

3 cups cooked or canned pink
    or light-red kidney beans,
    drained
3 cups cooked or canned
    garbanzos, drained
2 cups cooked or canned small
    white or navy beans, drained

1 cup coarsely chopped sweet
    pickles
½ cup drained, chopped
    pimientos
Sweet-and-Sour Dressing
    (below)

In a large salad bowl toss all the ingredients together, cover, and refrigerate overnight or longer. Pour off excess sauce before serving.

SERVES 8 to 10

Sweet-and-Sour Dressing

⅔ cup firmly packed light
    brown sugar
2 tablespoons cornstarch
¼ teaspoon black pepper
1 teaspoon salt
1 slice peeled yellow onion,
    finely minced

1 small clove garlic, finely
    minced
½ cup cold water
1½ cups boiling water
⅔ cup vinegar from sweet
    pickles, or white wine
    vinegar

In a small saucepan combine all the ingredients except the water and vinegar. Add the cold water and mix to a smooth consistency. Over low heat stir in boiling water and simmer, stirring constantly, until the mixture is thick and clear. Stir in the vinegar, then remove from heat.

YIELDS about 2⅔ cups

Mixed Bean Casserole with Ham

This recipe combines leftover cooked ham with garbanzos, dark red kidney beans, and small white beans.

*1 to 2 cups cooked diced ham,
   including some fat*
*1 large clove garlic, peeled and
   minced*
*1 large yellow onion, peeled and
   chopped*
*2 cups cooked or canned dark
   red kidney beans, drained*
*2 cups cooked or canned
   garbanzos, drained*
*2 cups cooked or canned small
   white beans, drained*

2 tablespoons prepared mustard
½ cup catsup
*½ cup dry white wine or 3
   tablespoons white vinegar
   plus ¼ cup water*
⅛ cup maple syrup (optional)
*1 tablespoon firmly packed
   dark brown sugar*
1 teaspoon salt
⅛ teaspoon black pepper
⅛ teaspoon ground cloves

1. Heat the oven to 350°F.
2. Sauté the diced ham in a large saucepan until the fat begins to melt. If there is little fat on the ham, add 2 tablespoons bacon drippings. Sauté the garlic and the onion with the ham until the onion is translucent. Add the remaining ingredients and combine thoroughly. If the mixture seems dry, add more catsup and more wine. Taste and add more salt and pepper if desired. Turn into a 2½-quart casserole and bake for 45 minutes.

SERVES 6

Black Beans and More Beans

This recipe comes from Saint Croix in the Virgin Islands. It can be made with canned snap beans or cooked fresh snap beans, or even cooked frozen snap beans. It will keep well in the refrigerator, covered, for about 2 weeks.

2 cups cooked French-cut green beans, drained

2 cups cooked cut wax beans, drained

2 cups cooked or canned black beans, drained

2 cups cooked or canned blackeye beans, drained

2 cups cooked or canned light red kidney beans, drained

1 cup cooked or canned baby limas, drained

1 can bean sprouts, drained

1 cup thin radish slices

2 cups minced red onion

2 cups minced seeded green pepper

1 cup sliced stuffed olives

2 cups broken cauliflower flowerets

½ cup thinly sliced gherkins

8 water chestnuts, sliced thin

1 small jar minced pimiento

1 can bamboo shoots, drained and slivered

1 small bottle capers, drained

⅔ cup tarragon vinegar

⅔ cup honey

1 cup vegetable oil

⅔ cup minced chutney and liquid

1 teaspoon sea salt

1 cup dark rum

In a huge bowl combine all the ingredients and toss well. Cover and chill before serving.

SERVES 25 to 30

Antipasto Supper

This is a supper of hors d'oeuvres, bits and ends of leftovers combined with tasty turnouts from cans. Serve it for late supper parties with crisp hot garlic bread and wine.

½ cup olive oil
½ cup vegetable oil
⅙ cup red wine vinegar
½ teaspoon dry mustard
½ teaspoon granulated sugar
2 to 4 teaspoons salt
½ teaspoon black pepper
2 cups cooked or canned light
    red kidney beans, drained
2 cups cooked or canned
    garbanzos, drained
1 teaspoon tarragon
1 large can mushroom caps,
    drained
1 package frozen artichoke
    hearts, cooked and drained
1 cup cooked diced beef
2 large yellow onions, peeled
    and finely minced

½ cup finely minced parsley
2 large ripe tomatoes, sliced
¼ cup finely minced basil
1 large can sardines in oil,
    drained
1 head chicory, washed and
    dried
1 garlic sausage, sliced
1 can colossal ripe olives,
    drained
1 can anchovies in oil, drained
1 small jar pimientos, drained
2 large sweet peppers, seeded
    and cut into strips
Crema Dania or Swiss
    cheese, sliced

1. Combine in the blender the olive oil, vegetable oil, vinegar, mustard, sugar, salt, and pepper and blend well. Taste and add more salt if desired.

2. Combine beans with ⅓ cup of the dressing in a large bowl. Cover and chill.

3. Mix tarragon with ¼ cup dressing. Warm the mushroom caps and artichoke hearts slightly in a little saucepan, drain, then toss with the tarragon-flavored dressing. Cover and set aside.

4. Combine beef with ⅛ cup dressing, 1 tablespoon minced onion, and 1 tablespoon parsley. Cover and chill.

5. Spread the tomato slices out on a plate, dribble a little dressing over each, and sprinkle with minced basil. Cover and set aside.

6. Arrange the sardines sides by side on a large plate, sprinkle with the remaining onion, and cover with remaining minced parsley. Cover and set aside.

7. Pour any dressing that remains over the beans, toss, and return to refrigerator.

8. Assemble the antipasto plate by lining a platter with chicory, frilly edges facing outward. Heap the beans in the center and arrange mushrooms, artichokes, beef, tomatoes, sardines, and garlic sausage slices around the beans. Garnish with olives, anchovies, pimiento slices, and pepper strips and edge with cheese slices.

SERVES 6 to 8

Green Beans Panache

This is a takeoff on a French bean dish that mixes green beans with the famous *flageolets*.

1 pound fresh green snap beans	*Salt to taste*
2 cups fresh baby lima beans	*4 tablespoons butter or margarine*
4 quarts rapidly boiling water	*½ teaspoon minced parsley*

1. Wash the green beans and snip off the stems and tips.

2. Place the lima beans in the rapidly boiling water, bring the water back to a boil, cover, lower the heat and simmer 15 minutes. Raise the heat so water returns to a rapid boil. Add the green beans a handful at a time. Bring the water back to a boil and cook the beans uncovered until tender, 15 to 20 minutes.

3. Drain, return to the heat, shake the saucepan to remove any remaining moisture, then add the salt and the butter or margarine. Garnish with parsley before serving.

SERVES 8 to 10

Beans and Beef Shanks

Dry limas or Great Northern beans can be used in place of the small white beans, and the speckled pintos can be substituted for light reds. Soak the small whites overnight before you begin (see pages 40–41 for soaking instructions).

⅔ cup (¼ pound) dry small white
    beans, soaked overnight
    (see pages 40–41)
⅔ cup (¼ pound) dry light red
    or pinto beans
3 cups cold water
2 tablespoons beef fat or
    vegetable oil
3 beef shank cross cuts (2 to
    2½ pounds)
1 large yellow onion, peeled
    and coarsely chopped

2 teaspoons granulated sugar
⅛ teaspoon crushed red pepper
2 tablespoons butter or
    margarine
2 tablespoons all-purpose flour
1 16-ounce can whole tomatoes
2 teaspoons salt
2 cups raw, canned, or frozen
    green snap beans
Salt and black pepper to taste

1. Wash the dry beans, pick them over, and place them in a large Dutch oven or a heavy kettle with a lid. Add the cold water and bring to a boil, uncovered; boil 2 minutes, remove from the heat, cover, and let stand for 1 hour.

2. Heat the fat or oil in a saucepan over high heat and quickly brown the shanks on all sides. Place the shanks in the Dutch oven, wedging them down into the beans, and add the onion, sugar, and red pepper. Cover and bring to a boil over medium heat. Reduce the heat and simmer for 2½ hours. Stir occasionally and add more water if the dish is drying out.

3. Melt the butter or margarine in a medium saucepan over medium low heat. Stir in the flour quickly, until smooth. Add the tomatoes and salt, stirring quickly so that no lumps form. Let mixture come to a simmer, stir until sauce has thickened, stir in the green beans, bring back to a boil, then mix into the beef mixture. Cover and continue cooking another 15 minutes. Add pepper and more salt if needed.

SERVES 6

Bean, Beef, and Peanut Stew

This is based on an African dish—a thick, hearty soup that's great with crusty hot rolls and a salad. Soak the small white beans overnight or by the quick-soak method (see pages 40–41 for soaking instructions) before you begin.

3 tablespoons butter or margarine
2 cups thinly sliced carrots
1 pound lean ground beef
3 quarts cold water
1 cup dry blackeye beans
1 cup dry small white beans, soaked overnight or by the quick-soak method (pages 40–41)
1 cup dry small lima beans

½ green pepper, minced
⅛ teaspoon crushed red pepper
1 cup peanut butter
2 tablespoons minced yellow onion
1 teaspoon dried basil
1½ teaspoon ground coriander
2 teaspoons salt
2 tablespoons minced fresh parsley

1. Melt the butter or margarine in a large Dutch oven or heavy kettle, add the carrots and the beef, and cook over medium high heat, stirring, until the beef is well browned. Add the water and scrape up the pan juices. Then add blackeye beans, soaked small whites, limas, green pepper and red pepper. Bring to a boil, stir, reduce the heat, cover, and simmer until the beans are tender, about 2 hours. Stir occasionally and add more water if needed.

2. Place the peanut butter in a medium bowl and stir in some of the broth. Add the onion, basil, and coriander. Add to the Dutch oven, then add the salt, stir, cover, and cook another 10 to 15 minutes. Taste and add more salt if needed. Sprinkle with parsley before serving.

SERVES 8 to 10

Hawaiian Dinner Soup with Seven Beans

Here's an economy measure: Save steak or beef roast bones in the freezer instead of buying soup bones to use in this soup. The dish tastes best when it is made the day before serving. With a salad and dessert it makes a complete meal. To get a head start, cook the pork hocks and soup bones 10 to 12 hours or overnight in a slow cooker (use ⅓ less water on the low-heat setting), and use canned beans and their canning liquids. If end result is too liquid, boil down, uncovered. If too dry, add beef bouillon.

4 small pork hocks
1 pound soup bones
5 cups dry beans: 1 cup navy, ⅔ cup each pinto, cranberry, kidney, blackeye, garbanzo, and lima beans
5 quarts cold water
1 tablespoon salt
¼ teaspoon pepper
1 large clove garlic, peeled and minced

5 medium yellow onions, peeled and minced
5 medium carrots, peeled and minced
5 medium stalks celery, with leaves, minced
1 16-ounce can whole tomatoes, chopped
1 garlic sausage (hot)

1. Wash the hocks, place them in a large kettle with the soup bones, and measure water to cover; add half again as much water. Cover, bring to a boil, and simmer 2½ hours.

2. While the hocks and bones cook, place the beans in a large kettle with 5 quarts water, salt, pepper, and garlic. Cover and cook until tender, about 2 hours. If beans run short of water, take some from the meat stock. If beans take longer to cook, turn the heat off under the hocks till beans are done. Remove the meat from the hocks, chop fine, and return to the stock. Discard hock and soup bones.

3. Add minced vegetables and tomatoes to the meat stock, along with the beans and bean liquid, and set to simmer. Meanwhile slice sausage into rounds ¼ inch thick, pan-fry till lightly browned, and add to soup. Simmer about 30 minutes more.

SERVES 10 to 12

Appendix

SOURCES OF GARDEN SEEDS

Alberta Nurseries & Seeds Ltd., Bowden, Altoona, Canada, TOM OKO. Gives away a colorful 35-page catalog. Seeds and plant varieties offered have been carefully chosen for adaptability to high altitudes and the short, cold, growing seasons of the Pacific Northwest and Canada.

Beale's Famous Products, Box 323, Ft. Washington, Pennsylvania 19034. Assortment of 15 different seeds in small test packages.

Garden Way Associates, 509 Westport Avenue, Norwalk, Connecticut 06851. Produces the Country Kitchen catalog annually. Included in it are hard-to-find food preserving tools, such as bean cutters and food dehydrators. Great browsing for good gardeners.

George W. Park Seed Co., Inc., Greenwood, South Carolina 29647. Specializes in flower and vegetable seeds of first rate quality and gives away a handsome, full-color 123-page catalog. Index of contents includes valuable information on germination time and best use. Cultural instructions are included for each kind.

Henry Field Seed & Nursery Co., Shenandoah, Iowa 51602. Gives away their excellent spring (117 pages) and fall (43 pages) catalogs.

J. A. Demonchaux Company, Inc., 827 North Kansas, Topeka, Kansas 66608.

Johnny's Selected Seeds, Organic Seed and Crop Research, Albion, Maine 04910. Charges $.50 for their 48-page black-and-white catalog but refunds the amount with the first order. Their specialty is organically grown seed they raise themselves: other seeds are high quality, often imported (Oriental food plant seeds from Japan, etc.).

Le Jardin du Gourmet, West Danville, Vermont 05873. A catalog available that barely qualifies as one, though there's a $.25 charge for it. However, it's the place to look for cooking specialties such as shallots and French bean and vegetable seeds—*mache* (corn salad), sorrel, salsify, et al. Imported truffles, snails, and what-have-you are included.

Natural Development Company, Bainbridge, Pennsylvania 17502. Organically-grown seeds, including bush limas and edible green soybeans.

Nichols Garden Nursery, 1190 North Pacific Highway, Albany, Oregon 97321.

The Organic Directory, Rodale Press, Emmaus, Pennsylvania 18049. This is a source book for all organic food suppliers.

Redwood City Seed Company, P.O. Box 361, Redwood City, California 94064. Sells a small (24-page) catalog for $.25. Plants they consider useful are offered, including some wild ancestors of common food plants. Fun to browse through, since the book includes things like carob tree seeds and soybeans.

Shiloh Farms, Route 59, Sulphur Springs, Arkansas 72768. Catalog available, but they sell mostly wholesale.

Walnut Acres, Penns Creek, Pennsylvania 17862. All kinds of seeds and grains. Interesting free catalog.

W. Atlee Burpee Company, Box 748, 6350 Rutland Avenue, Riverside, California 92502. Gives away a giant 180-page full color catalog of seeds and everything for the garden. Famous for pioneering work in introducing hybrids. Burpee's is one of America's leading seedsmen.

General Index

Index of Recipes